IN LIMBO *too*

BREXIT TESTIMONIES FROM
UK CITIZENS IN THE EU

IN LIMBO too

BREXIT TESTIMONIES FROM UK CITIZENS IN THE EU

From an idea by **Elena Remigi**

Foreword by Prof. A.C. Grayling

Edited by
Elena Remigi, Debbie Williams, Helen De Cruz, Sarah Pybus,
Clarissa Killwick and Paul Blackburn

CONTENTS

FOREWORD

Of all the many wrongs that constitute Brexit one of the worst is the betrayal of those who have come to Britain from our partner countries in the EU, and those British who have gone to our partner countries in the EU, to make their lives. In many cases these are people who not only work and pay their taxes in their adopted parts of the European Union, but who have married citizens of their new places of domicile, have brought children into the world there, have established careers and friendships there – in short: have made their homes and committed themselves to their futures there. The Brexit referendum has ripped away their security, overturned their worlds, treated them with utter disrespect even to the point of publicly and explicitly describing them as 'pawns' in a negotiation. I am ashamed of my country that this has happened. I am anguished at the thought of the uncertainty, anxiety, misery and grief this causes so many of my fellow European citizens. I would not have believed anyone who told me, before this actually happened, that my own country was capable of behaving in such a crass and revolting way. Yet it has happened.

The nature and degree of this betrayal merits exploration, for it says something about the forces that are antipathetic to the ideals of the EU. Let us acknowledge that the EU has its flaws and problems; no-one knows this better than those in the European Commission and Parliament who work to help this great, imaginative and progressive project address its difficulties and move towards its goal. That goal is to create a unity of nations dedicated to peace, security and material well-being for all its peoples, with their civil liberties protected and their varied and various cultures respected, celebrated and enjoyed. It is a co-operative enterprise, the creation of a shared Europe-wide homeland in which all the great benefits of scale can be harvested for everyone's good.

Who would oppose such a thing? What is it that motivates a rejection of this aim in preference for a narrow, nationalistic, divisive, self-regarding localism that does not want to pool resources and co-operate, given the manifest advantages of doing so? In my view one of the main things to blame is the ambition of a certain kind of politician. At the crudest level this ambition is not to cede anything to shared responsibility, but to be in control; not to be a small frog in a big pond but a big frog in a small pond. In pursuit of this, such politicians find it convenient to distort the truth, even to lie about, the EU; they find it convenient to stoke xenophobic feelings, to blame 'Brussels' and foreigners for problems most of which are in truth the result of local political failings.

This is deeply regrettable, not only because the social and economic progress of the EU as a whole is challenged by it, but because so many Europeans have benefitted in personal ways from the freedom to travel, live and work across the whole of our shared continent, forming relationships and putting down roots, and in the vast majority of cases contributing vitally and materially to the countries in which they have thus made their homes.

We must not forget that the Brexit situation which is causing this uncertainty and unhappiness is highly questionable from a constitutional point of view. The referendum was an explicitly advisory exercise, in which only 37% of those who were granted a vote used it in support of leaving the EU. I use the words 'who were granted a vote': the electorate enfranchised for the referendum deliberately excluded three important constituencies of people with a very material interest in the outcome, namely, citizens of other EU countries resident in Britain, expatriates who had been abroad for fifteen years or more, and 16-17 years olds. And this leaves aside many other questions that have been raised about the Leave campaign's activities and their bearing on the referendum's validity. Yet the government of the UK has treated the referendum as if it constituted a mandate, and accordingly, without proper consideration, have placed those of our fellow EU citizens who live among us as our neighbours, friends, lovers, spouses and colleagues, into limbo: the limbo of an undeserved, unfair and callous treatment of them as pawns in the Brexit negotiations.

As I write these words the UK is still in the EU. I believe that its future will always be in the EU, whether in the shorter or the longer term. But in the meantime the disgraceful treatment of our fellow EU citizens continues. What it means to be thrust into limbo, to feel rejected, to have one's life turned upside down by the Brexit process, is poignantly and upsettingly described in the contributions in these pages. Our fellow citizens have a great claim on our sense of solidarity and support: in the spirit of the EU itself we must combine with them to right this wrong, to defend them and their interests, to reject the ugly spirit that treats them in this outrageous way. I repeat: they are our neighbours, friends, lovers, spouses and colleagues: the Brexiter politicians may have thrust them into limbo, but their true place is in our hearts and friendship, as fellow citizens, now and always.

Professor A.C. Grayling CBE

INTRODUCTION

In Limbo Too is a powerful not-for-profit collection of testimonies from UK citizens living in other EU countries during the Brexit process. It captures the shame, anger, fear, and worries of real people in their own voices and shows them as unique individuals rather than anonymous statistics or stereotypes. It is the sequel to *In Limbo*, a volume with testimonies of EU citizens living in the UK. That book told the stories of people who were no longer sure if they could call the UK their home, and who felt betrayed in the trust they had, both in the government and in their local communities.

The present collection tells the story of British citizens in the EU, including some testimonies from citizens living in the EEA, who are equally in limbo. In many respects, EU citizens in the UK and UK citizens in the EU are each other's mirror image. Both groups of citizens face considerable uncertainty. Their rights are on the negotiating table, together with trade, the Irish border, and a host of other issues. Given that their continued rights to reside, work, and have access to public services in the EU are still not conclusively agreed (at the time of publication), their lives are on hold. In public discussions on citizens' rights, the personal cost is often forgotten.

This work is the result of the intimate collaboration and partnership between two groups "In Limbo-Our Brexit Testimonies" (IL-OBT) and "Brexpats Hear Our Voice" (BHOV), created respectively for EU nationals living in the UK and British citizens living in Europe, who all have concerns about the impact of Brexit on their future. The project originated in 2017 when Elena Remigi opened a Facebook group called "Our Brexit Testimonies" with the aim of creating a book by collecting testimonies from EU citizens living in the UK. At the time when *In Limbo* was published, it was clear we needed a second volume to capture the complexities and the human cost of Brexit for UK citizens who have made one of the EU-27 countries their home. The majority of British citizens came to the European continent under freedom of movement, and took their rights as EU citizens for granted. Now they live in uncertainty. An overarching theme that unifies these testimonies is how Brexit has ripped apart not only a nation, but also extended families, spanning several countries. Friendships have been broken, family relations are tense. As one testimony puts it "My [leave-voting] Dad is a party to this and it's hard to forgive." or "I wrestle daily with the knowledge that half of my family in England voted Leave. I know they didn't vote to hurt me, but still the pain is almost physical."

There are feelings of bereavement, loss and sadness. One particular feeling that British citizens have been experiencing is shame, expressed in several testimonies. Not because of anything they personally did, but because of the vote to leave the EU, and the way the UK government has acted since that vote. As stated by some, they felt proud to be British when London hosted the Olympic Games in 2012. Now they feel disillusionment and shame. As one author put it "Until the referendum I considered myself an expat, but in 2016 something happened to my beloved homeland. It was split asunder, now taken over by those who oppose everything I value about it, and who despise my fellow Europeans living there. It truly does break my heart to see this happening."

When Theresa May called people who self-identify as citizens of the world "citizens of nowhere", these British citizens felt this as a personal rejection and as a governmental repudiation of their multi-layered identity: "And yet, right now, as a Brit in Europe I do feel like a citizen of nowhere. My own government doesn't care about the likes of me. We have been disenfranchised, abandoned, abused even." The issue of identity is complex. Another common theme throughout these testimonies is a sense of a loss of identity, and being forced to choose between different aspects of one's identity. Some of our authors feel primarily an emotional attachment to their country of residence, for example: "I don't have a British accent. I see myself as European. A European Brit. My identity has disappeared. I feel vulnerable, I feel I no longer belong anywhere. This was my home and my life". Others saw the different identities as more equal, for example, "I feel as British as I do Scottish as I do European and am sick of being told I have to choose between the nationalities I was born with." Others, again, feel decidedly British, for instance "Whilst I love where I live, very fond of the inhabitants and really value being in central Europe, I don't feel at all German. I feel totally British. I don't even want to have dual citizenship – but I may have to." In fact, for many, obtaining citizenship seems their only option to safeguard the freedom of movement essential to their mainland European lives; to do so, however, is fraught with difficulties and sometimes impossible.

Following the EU Referendum, the UK government unilaterally refused to guarantee the right of EU citizens to stay in the UK. First, they claimed EU citizens were to be *bargaining chips*, whose rights should be haggled over at the negotiating table rather than ring-fenced at the outset. Then they argued that EU citizens should be *human shields*, to be used to protect UK citizens in the EU. In this way, two groups of citizens were pitted against each other, in a stark zero-sum game whereby loss of one group of citizens' rights would automatically result in a reduction of rights of the other group. But as a consequence, UK citizens in the EU also became bargaining chips and human shields too. We want to combine our voices as UK citizens in Europe with those of our friends and colleagues, the EU citizens in Britain, so that we can no longer be collectively ignored or marginalised. We need to get these testimonies out to decision makers across Europe to shape the debate and remind them that we are real people. We also want to make sure that the wider public has access to both books and hear our combined voice through our personal testimonies.

In our editing, we wanted to retain the authentic, diverse voices, and so we have only made minor corrections for typos, as well as some shortening or cutting some digressions. There were many more submissions than we had space to accommodate. Like *In Limbo*, the structure of the book is built on feelings. Each section has a prevalent emotional "flavour", but feelings are often intermingled so it is never clear-cut.

It is unclear what the outcome of the negotiations will be. Even if all is be settled, and we will "only" face the reduction of some rights we enjoyed before, the emotional cost will remain. We hope that these testimonies will demolish stereotypes about what UK citizens in the EU are like, and that they will highlight the cost of Brexit for citizens—the cost in terms of loss of earnings, in terms of a loss of a sense of identity, a loss of trust in the UK government, a loss of family and friends. We also hope that these powerful voices will go some way to countering the narrative of 'you chose, you moved, deal with it' to show the complexity of each individual's situation. As one person sums up the aim of this collection of testimonies: "Please remember, I'm not a statistic, 1 of 1.2 million; I'm not just words on a page and I'm definitely not a political bargaining chip. I'm a scared young woman, who had just started building up her life when the foundations were pulled away."

The editors of In Limbo Too

A LITTLE NOTE ABOUT THE COVER

When Article 50 was triggered, Dante's words came to my mind:

> *"Nel mezzo del cammin di nostra vita*
> *mi ritrovai in una selva oscura*
> *ché la diritta via era perduta"*

They translate into English as:

> "Midway upon the journey of our life,
> I found myself in a forest dark,
> For the straight path had been lost"

(Dante, *Inferno*, Canto I)

These wonderful lines inspired not only the title of the original *In Limbo* book, but also – later on and quite uncannily – its cover.

When Gareth Harrey decided to help us with the design of the cover, we told him that we wanted to express the situation of limbo that many people were facing.

Gareth's cover truly represented our limbo: a place of uncertainty, sadness, confusion, fragility, and many other painful feelings. I felt that the cover of *In Limbo Too* designed by Gareth's daughter Alice should be consistent with that of the first book, but must also complement and develop it.

In times such as these, it is worth remembering that the chalk hills of Kent, that end so abruptly at the white cliffs of Dover, are the selfsame chalk hills that rise up again on the other side of the Channel, with the white cliffs of France stretching from Calais to Boulogne. There was still land connecting Britain with continental Europe before it was swept away by a devastating tsunami in 6,100 BC.

In 2018 we are trying to make sense of a new tsunami that threatens to separate Britain from her neighbours. *In Limbo Too* adds the voices of the 1.2 million UK citizens living in the European Union to those of the 3.6 million EU citizens living in Britain. The iconography and design of both the book-covers taken together offers not only the image of the individual seeking a way out from the dark forest, but a broader narrative of a host of men, women and children looking for a path among the trees. As the cover of *In Limbo Too* reflects with its powerful colouring, they are searching together for the deep blue sea beyond the gloom and the clear blue sky against which the stars shine so brightly; to look across at each other from the cliff-tops on both sides of the water, calling out, reaching out, eschewing separation, seeking connection.

Indeed, Dante's *Inferno* ends with the verse:

"E quindi uscimmo a riveder le stelle"
"Thence we came forth to re-behold the stars"

(Dante, *Inferno*, Canto XXXIV)

This is my wish for each one of us. Our limbo is not only about whether we have the right documents to be able to live in the country that we call home. There is a psychological limbo too, into which we have been plunged. My hope is that we can all "re-behold the stars", as content and settled as we first were before this Referenum.

Elena Remigi

A STORY

A PERSONAL REFLECTION ON SOVEREIGNTY

It seems that in Brexit Britain, sovereignty trumps all: economics, community, global standing, even seventy years of peace. Self-determination has stood at the centre of the drive for Britain to leave the EU. Millions of citizens still have their hearts set on what they imagine to be a repatriated sovereignty in spite of a growing public awareness of the economic, legal, social, diplomatic and political costs of Brexit.

Looking back over my own life, my personal 'sovereignty' was at its height during a period in the late '70s and early '80s. I was in my twenties, a street musician travelling through Europe, playing a town a day. I slept in the back of my old estate car, and lived out of a rucksack. No wife, no kids, no girlfriend, no employer. Footloose, fancy-free, the life of Larry. With no commitments to anything or to anybody, and with no constraints beyond the Law and my own morality, my self-determination was complete.

During that time, something started to change. I remember awaking one morning from a powerful dream as I lay in my sleeping-bag in the back of the car, parked up in some provincial European town. In the dream, I had become the father to a child, and I awoke brimming with emotion. It was early, and the car park was still empty. After a wash and breakfast in the local supermarket, I played the morning busking shift, feeling unsettled by the dream in a town centre that seemed bizarrely full of expectant young mothers. The dream marked the beginning of the end of that itinerant life, tectonic plates were shifting deep inside. I began to long for a wife, for children, for a hearth and home. From across the span of decades, I can now see that I was longing for an ending to my sovereignty and separateness, and for a beginning to commitment and connection.

When I met my wife, not long afterwards, I gladly relinquished large slices of my old sovereignty. Before long our two children arrived, and how I loved those babies who clipped my carefree wings so comprehensively. Having committed to a mortgage on our first house and to an employer with my freshly-donned suit and tie, another slice of sovereignty slipped away. When after some years I went independent, my clients were as demanding of my commitment as my employers had been. In that grown-up life, I paid my taxes, drove the kids around, attended the in-laws' birthday parties, went to the weddings, went to the funerals, and on Saturday morning cast a grateful coin into a busker's case. As my sovereignty drained away, my life became richer, our lives became richer. As we commit to others, to laws, to rules, to agreements, to family, to friends, to employers, to customers, and to broader groups and communities, our sovereignty erodes. The loss of sovereignty is the price of connection and commitment. We say yes to it. When we hear the Brexit Evangelists preaching their message of sovereignty, they are not appealing to the developed adult in us, they speak not to the mature men and women who have understood the relationship between sovereignty and commitment, but rather they appeal to the young adventurer in us, to the unfledged, the non-committal, the irresponsible and the egocentric. "If the cap fits...", and it seems that for millions of Britons, this cap fits very nicely.

I would not have missed my wild-oats years for the world, nor would I have missed the more onerous richness that ensued. Looking at the history of this nation, it occurs to me that Britain should not be regressing into nostalgic buccaneering but should rather retain its seat amongst the adult nations that set an example to and facilitate the coming-of-age of the less developed ones. From that dignified station we have now, alas, retreated. Perhaps in years to come, this nation will awake one morning in its centrally-locked British-built estate car in a lonely corner of the global car park, prisoner of its own freedom, castaway on its own sceptred isle, longing not for the richness it dreams of for but for the richness it has thrown away.

Adrian Hackford, England

PART I

"I feel isolated and alone"

Watching, waiting, and hurting. That's how it feels to be in limbo. Watching from a distance as the UK severs its bonds with the rest of Europe and waiting, horrified, as it unravels our union. Instead of a United Kingdom, rich in all our diversity, we are becoming an Untied Kingdom, unfastened from the values that once held us together, and scurrying into dark corners to bleat. There's little I can do from here. I write to politicians, give money and send messages of support to those that speak for me. I have no voice myself. That right was taken away when I passed the fifteen-year threshold I am living in Spain where the sun shines longer and stronger than elsewhere. But I came here to do a job, and that job was to promote British culture and British education of which I was once so proud. Now though, I'm not so sure. There is so much to learn by being open to other cultures and Brexit will close down those opportunities for the very generations we should be serving. How can they stand on our shoulders if we are stooped so low? I am still proud to be British in some unreasoned, emotional way but now I am 100% European and fully embrace all those values that good people in the European Commission are striving to achieve.

What hurts most is the lack of understanding about the European Union by the public. Very often my British family, friends and acquaintances throw up inaccurate and often critical generalisations about the EU that bear no relation to the day-to-day reality of living in a modern European community. I could list the benefits but is it my job to do so? Surely the politicians should have done that, years ago. I could also list the ways in which I will be affected on a personal level and there are many. But this is an issue that stretches beyond the personal and idiosyncratic. And so I watch, wait and hurt: angered by the self-interest of inadequate politicians and by the partisan press who fuel the fire of dissension just to make a profit.

Patricia, Spain

★★★

In 2015, I had the opportunity to study abroad for a semester in France. Little did I know how much my life would change as a result... Prior to this experience, I considered myself an open-minded person, but in reality I only saw things from the perspective that I'd grown up with back home. I'd only ever been to two countries outside the UK and though I was good at languages at school, I could only speak English fluently.

Thanks to the EU's Erasmus programme, as a UK citizen I was able to move to France with relative ease by not needing a visa and not needing to register for social security – things which non-EU nationals had a lot of difficulty dealing with. I also received a generous study grant to support me financially during my time abroad. In the city of Nantes, I got to experience a new life in many ways. I experienced a different life at university, improved my career prospects and met some friends that I will hold onto for life. I not only gained an appreciation of living abroad, but also of the UK – my home. I felt a real sense of pride to recognise how influential, well-respected and advanced my country was in the world, and I felt proud to be representing my country to others.

Today, I'm writing this testimony from Marseille, as I study for an International Business and Corporate Finance masters double degree, thanks to a partnership between a UK University and a French Business School. I can now speak 3 languages fluently and 2 others conversationally, and I could now launch my career in one of several European countries. I've visited most of Western Europe, ventured across the water to the US and the French Caribbean, and also spent a summer in Barcelona after arriving and successfully finding a job there.

A lot of these life decisions and the achievements that have come as a result can be credited to those first three months studying abroad on the Erasmus programme. It helped me to develop my cultural awareness, confidence and an open-minded approach – skills that have helped me get to where I am today, and that are becoming increasingly important in a world that is becoming more closely integrated.

Brexit threatens the future of many UK nationals living within the EU, including me, but also the people of my generation living in the UK who may not get the same opportunities that I had going forward. Every day I read the news, I ask myself about what my rights will look like after Brexit Day. I ask myself whether employers in the EU will reject me from future job opportunities because of my nationality. I ask myself about the opportunities my generation will miss out on because of possibly withdrawing from the Erasmus agreement. It is saddening to watch my country turn its back on the EU – an institution that positively impacted the lives of many, despite its flaws. I can't accept that my own future, or the futures of a considerable number of fellow UK citizens will be compromised as a result of Brexit.

Jonny, Masters student, France

Somewhere in the North East of Italy... I was dashing between teaching jobs, and just had time to drop into a bar for a hot chocolate. I checked my phone, and saw a post from a British friend, who lives in another EU country. She was describing the pain of the damaged relationship with her in-laws in the UK who voted Leave. This was my hurried comment, before disappearing up into the hills to get to my next student:

"With some family and friends I felt that, all of a sudden, I was speaking a different language. One told me that I had voted with my feet by leaving. It has changed my relationship even with people I don't know. When I visit the UK, I don't want to look people in the eye. I feel we are considered an inferior class. One relationship has improved though.

My mum originally told me that I was overreacting and it was bad for me... now I think she is proud I am fighting."

I am still feeling alienated by my country for being British somewhere else.

Anonymous, Italy

★★★

Science is international. A message that surrounded me from the moment I started my PhD, as a British student at a British university, in 2000. In part, it is about money; cutting-edge telescopes and experiments are expensive, and often require international collaboration. But it is more than that. Being open to the exchange of new ideas and ways of looking at a problem, working together to understand the Universe – is part and parcel of what it means to be a scientist.

I was steeped in this culture from the beginning. My PhD advisor was Swedish. Group members came from Austria, France, Germany, Greece, Italy and beyond. We were part of an EU research network that led to regular workshops and exchanges. I made friends with young scientists at other European universities, many of whom are now faculty colleagues at universities around the world.

It was understood that a career in astrophysics would require at least one or two postdoctoral positions abroad. I moved to the USA, and then to Germany, marvelling at how much simpler the administration was when moving within the EU. Then to the Netherlands, ostensibly for a short-term position. That was ten years ago. My husband and I were offered faculty positions here. Our two amazing bilingual children were born here. We made friends. It has become home.

My work continues to be embedded in the European framework. My

PhD students and postdoctoral researchers come from all over the EU. My research is funded by the European Research Council. And I am part of a European Consortium working to build the next generation of X-ray space telescopes. My work takes me all over the continent, and I count myself lucky indeed to work with such a wonderful group of scientists and engineers.

Brexit is anathema to everything that I stand for as a scientist, and since the referendum I have been through all the stages of grief, anger, and – occasionally – resignation. The UK government has shown complete disregard for the welfare of British citizens in the EU27, the Embassy has provided little to no useful advice, and the intervening months have rammed home to me just how vulnerable we are. I took the Dutch integration ('*Inburgering*') exams last year, and applied for citizenship for myself and my children in December. If my application is approved I will have to relinquish my British citizenship as a result. My Dutch friends have asked me if I find will find this upsetting, and that is a difficult question to answer. In some ways, yes, I will always take milk in my tea and form a queue of one! But in other ways, no, it is the easiest choice in the world. I am a European scientist; my life and work have been immeasurably enriched by the chance to move freely across the continent. Denying my children the opportunities that I have been given is simply not an option.

Anna Watts, the Netherlands

I "deserted a sinking ship", "voted with my feet", "abandoned the UK"... these are just some of the things that have been said to me by British family, friends and, of course, complete strangers since we moved here in 1994, (from a large industrial city in England to a very small Greek island, where I still live, very happily). No one was really interested that we pay tax on all our UK income and receive nothing in return.

Not even a Vote.

I was saddened by the negative comments, and am unsurprised at the current prevailing attitude, downgrading us to second class citizens. No vote, no voice. It seems that the British government are happy to take my money in taxation, with all the responsibilities of Citizenship without any of the rights. I'm actually very hurt and angry that people who actually know me are happy to join in the bullying, it is diminishing.

L.S., Greece

★★★

After 33 years living, working and studying in the south of the Netherlands – as well as in neighbouring Belgium and Germany – I've clocked up a lot of European mileage. But even though I speak fluent Dutch and adequate German and am fully integrated into my local community, I haven't morphed into a foreigner. I've always retained ties with friends and family in the UK, followed the fortunes of my local football club, Manchester United, from afar, but often close up, and even helped start a successful cricket club in the town where I live.

Embracing both a British and European identity has never presented a hindrance to me. Working as a full-time translator, my years of living on the Continent and my own cultural and linguistic background have given me a distinct insight into the subtle differences between source and target cultures, so that I am uniquely placed to take advantage of that profession. I also teach English and hope I have managed to dispel many of the stereotypes and contributed in a positive way to an understanding of British and English-speaking cultures, (even though that may come back to haunt me after Brexit).

Living on the continent, particularly at the crossroads of Dutch, German and French-speaking cultures, has been instrumental in accomplishing much on a personal and professional level, so yes, I feel as much European as I do British. Up until June 2016, I'd never questioned the fact that the two might be incompatible. Without doubt, the driving force behind that sense of duality has been the political alliance forged between the nation states of Europe, the erstwhile Common Market, now the European Union, an institution that has undisputedly helped keep the peace on the continent. After the outcome of the EU referendum that balance has been irrevocably upset.

Materially, I don't think my life is going to change significantly after Brexit but that doesn't stop me from feeling terribly angry and sad. When I do have to show my passport in the future I shall feel like second-class citizen of Europe. It's not just the ignominy of it, but the tangible loss of rights too. Only the other day I received a voting card for the council elections and thought: these could be the last I ever vote in? When we do leave the EU, the right to vote at local and European elections will be taken away from me, since dual nationality is not an option for me in the Netherlands. I now very much regret the fact that if I'd had the foresight to do so more than 10 years ago, I could have acquired Dutch nationality (alongside UK nationality) automatically when I was still married to my Dutch wife.

But most of all, I feel extremely sad that the rights we have enjoyed for most of our lives are now going to be denied to a younger, more open generation of Britons who do not share the same blinkered visions of the older ones. I still can't quite believe that anyone would want to sweep these rights away in this day and age – and I even hold close family members responsible for this! As an A-level language student in the 1970s, I thought joining the EU was fantastic. More than anything it broadened my horizons and opened up cultures that I never knew existed. So I worry about what kind of Europe our children and grandchildren will now face.

Andrew Davies, the Netherlands

★★★

My maternal grandmother was born in the German Empire under the Kaiser. When she was five years old, her town was separated from the rest of Germany by the so-called "Danzig corridor." When she was 18 the fledgling democracy she had grown up in had transformed itself into the Third Reich. By the time she reached 31, the Soviet Army had captured her town and enacted summary revenge on its inhabitants for the horrors of the Nazi invasion. By the time she reached the age I am now, her family had been expelled and all had fled west, and she found herself in a displaced persons camp in Italy. Her town became part of Communist Poland and it wasn't until she was 75 that democracy returned to it. Full free movement between her birthplace and her home in the UK began the year before her death at the age of 91.

It is very difficult to comprehend such a huge degree of change in just one lifetime. The 20th Century was characterised by division; by wars, by fascism and communism, and iron curtains. The idea of a continent of free people able to live, work, trade, study and retire across its frontiers was impossible for so much of my grandmother's life. The creation of the European Union reflected a triumph of will over the past's inevitability of conflict. It's now possible to fly cheaply from London to Gdansk for the weekend, as if it were any other part of your country.

All of that is under threat. And not just on a practical level but – much more deeply – also on a theoretical level. The idea that we are all one people, separated simply by the accident of geographical place of birth, is receding. We are choosing to identify more and more with our immediate geography and to create and then exploit differences with other people born on different parts of the planet. There are no wins from this.

Seb Dance, UK

I'm Scottish and British and European, and I've lived in Belgium for 9 years working for the EU institutions. There isn't a huge amount of attention or sympathy for British Eurocrats, and certainly we're not the real story of Brexit. The rest of this book will tell you the impact it is having on people outside the 'Brussels bubble'; we don't pretend we are the worst-hit by this disaster. But we're devastated, and we have a story to tell.

In hindsight the referendum result was not a huge surprise, but it came as a shock. It has shattered every element of our lives and I have still not really come to terms with what it will mean for me. I'm passionately pro-European and planned a career in the EU institutions but since the result almost two years ago nothing has been clarified at all. I don't know if I will lose my job next year or not. Career options are being closed off as we become 3rd country nationals. I still have no idea if I will keep my right to free movement across the continent. Everything – my career, my legal right to residency, my citizenship, has been thrown up in the air. Thanks to my position as EU institution staff I have been outside the Belgian registration system, registered instead as an employee of an international organisation. This distinction was meaningless until the referendum, but now means I am not eligible to apply for Belgian citizenship, despite almost a decade of legal residence here. Various court cases at different levels of the Belgian state have returned different verdicts, so there is no clear way forward.

And who do I work for now? I feel as British as I do Scottish as I do European and am sick of being told I have to choose between the nationalities I was born with. The UK government has abandoned Brits on the continent, to the extent that we rely on the European Commission to defend our rights more than our own government. When the British tabloids scream about "saboteurs" and "enemies of the people" I can only imagine what they would say about me, a British national who works for and is loyal to the European Union. Being considered a traitor by your national press is horrible. All these years we Brits in the EU thought we were building something together, for a stronger continent, and by the time the sun rose on 24th June 2016, both the government and opposition had left us on our own. A large chunk of the British press would shrug at this and scoff that, of course, I'm devastated at Brexit, it means fat cats like me have to come off the gravy train. But I'm not pro-European because I work here. I chose to work here precisely because I'm pro-European. I had no preconceived notions of the EU before I started studying it over 15 years ago. But to me it was immediately both a practical and inspirational Union; a logical way for European countries to maximise their economic and political clout while also building a lasting peace which our continent had never known.

The shock that has reverberated with me and my colleagues has shown just how fragile the EU and its peace project is. After 40 years of UK membership I thought the EU foundation was strong, even during periods of flux. That the common institutions, policies and rights we had built up would endure. It was heartbreaking to see in one night, one desperate gamble to unite the Tory party, the whole house of cards came down and took us with it.

I've worked with politicians from all parties and all 28 Member States for the past 9 years and I probably have a higher-than-average respect for Members of Parliament. Most of them are decent, principled and hard-working individuals who fundamentally want to make things better for their constituents, their country and their continent. I see the pressure they are under by a rabid tabloid press and social media which is skittering out of control, and I admire their tenacity to calmly weigh up each vote and find the common good. It is because of my experience in the European Parliament and my respect for decent politicians that I harbour a deep disgust for the deceit the guilty men of Brexit pulled on our country. They gambled and lost the future of the UK on their political ambitions, they lied, and they will recklessly blame anyone but themselves for the crisis they have triggered. Their lack of basic EU knowledge is criminal. It has been truly staggering to watch the lies tumble out their mouths with sheer indifference. The impasse over the Irish border, Gibraltar, product standards, customs checks, Galileo, airline landing slots, rolling over EU trade agreements, medicines approval is nothing new. We know these policy areas, we work on them, we've been shouting for two years about the damage the UK is doing to itself. We will have to spend the next year reconciling Brexit with our future: our identity, job contracts, career prospects, nationality, families and relationships that now reach beyond the EU border. But we will never, ever forgive the guilty men of Brexit for what they have done. They can go whistle.

Jenni, Belgium

★★★

Elfriede and my mother had been penfriends before World War II and resumed that friendship afterwards despite, or perhaps because of, both having lost brothers in the war.

Much later as a student, I had the opportunity to go to Leipzig and met Elfriede. This was unusual in the early sixties, where East Berlin was as far as most Western visitors were allowed to go.

It was a memorable trip because of the insight it gave to me of life the other side of the Iron Curtain. The glimpse of East Germany that I had on that short trip included having it made clear to me that one definitely did not ask the hotel for an extra blanket and the tour guide in Weimar going round scraping up the leftover butter from our breakfast plates to take home.

Much later, my mother had an opportunity to meet Elfriede in East Berlin. Much later still, but soon enough after the Wall came down for the drive to the Baltic Coast from Berlin to have been in a Trabant, both couples went on holiday together and became firm friends, with Elfriede and Siegfried visiting my parents in the UK.

It is the little things that can affect a lifetime, and perhaps this one friendship is the reason I believe so strongly in the importance of the EU as a bulwark against conflict in Europe, resent so strongly that many of my compatriots cannot see how that transcends the undoubted imperfections of the EU, and feel so torn between the British and the European me.

M., France

★★★

I'm 19 and I was born in London. When I was one my mother lost her job, and my parents decided to try living in another European country. We moved to Italy and have stayed there ever since.

Until the referendum, I didn't really appreciate being European. My thoughts were stuck on my homeland, always thinking that life was better there than here. Now I feel a bit of an outsider. Never had I thought that the UK, a supposedly very open country, would be ignorant about the EU. I still can't describe the shock I felt the morning of the referendum results. I don't know whether I want to come back to the UK now.

Brexit threatens my voting rights, but I firmly believe that every vote counts, that everyone should have a vote and use it. I want to be a model of the kind of country I'd like to live in. I'm very lucky compared to others as, unintentionally, we've ended up in an EU country where dual citizenship is allowed. Right now, I'm only a British citizen, but I'm applying for Italian citizenship, to get back the rights I arrived with. I'm concerned about other "Brexpats", as they have to make a big decision on whether to give up their UK citizenship, or just hope nothing bad will happen. I hope there's a possibility the UK won't leave the EU, after all.

Brexit has opened my eyes. I'm more aware of history and politics. I think lack of education has been a key problem with Brexit. Talking to people my age in the UK, I'm shocked how little they know about history; statistics show that only around 40% of GCSE takers choose history. If you haven't really learnt about the two world wars, dictatorships in Italy, Germany and Russia, it's hard to understand the reason why the EU was created.

Previously I wanted to study in the UK but I'm currently applying to go to university in the Netherlands. The fees are lower, (about €2000 a year compared to £9000), and I've discovered the standard of education in the Netherlands is very high. At a university open day I was startled, but perhaps not surprised, to see Brexit in the presentations – a case study, devoid of the human perspective.

My biggest passions now are politics and music. I certainly would like to be in the music business. Part of me would still like to go back to the UK... I would like to support Remainers and campaign with them because I still care about the UK. But who knows, I might find opportunities elsewhere now.

Lewis Killwick-Vintner, Italy

★★★

I moved to Romania in 2002, five years before the country joined the EU. In those days, foreigners could only stay for 90 days at a time. The British School would run a minibus to Ruse, (in Bulgaria), and back every three months, to keep their teachers within the limit. I was once fined at the airport for overstaying.

After I met my Romanian partner, we had to queue overnight outside the British Embassy for him to get a visa to come and meet my family and friends in the UK. We joked that he was only with me because of my passport.

After 2007, everything changed. People could come and go freely. The ability to travel had a visible impact on Romanian society. There was more open-mindedness. Services improved. There was more money to spend. Having heard from my partner and friends how life was in a closed country, it felt like progress, like walls coming down.

When David Cameron promised a referendum on Britain's EU membership, my stomach turned over. However, I trusted him, that this was a tactical move like the referenda on AV and Scottish independence that he had won, a way to silence the Euro-sceptics and be able to move on. I thought he knew what he was doing.

I usually love watching election coverage. But as the first results came in on the night of June 23, I started to feel sick.

From that day on, it was a new landscape. My country, which I had thought was largely tolerant, where racism and bigotry were now pushed to the fringes, feels like a different place. The bigots are now in the ascendency, emboldened, gloating that their previously unacceptable views have been newly legitimised.

European citizens, who had built lives in the UK, expecting stability, contributing to our society, doing jobs that many Brits won't do, suddenly felt insecure, unwelcome. The UK, which enjoyed such a great reputation in Romania, is diminished, the lustre of the 2012 Olympics and our soft power tarnished by the resurgence of the far right and the xenophobia I thought was history.

My partner and I now have two children. Through him, they can acquire Romanian nationality, and therefore maintain their EU citizenship, which otherwise looks set to be stripped from them before they're even old enough to go to school. Theoretically, there may come a time when their mum and dad are no longer allowed to live in the same country as each other.

Now my partner and I joke that it's me who is with him for his passport, not the other way round. But it no longer seems funny.

D.S., Romania

★★★

I look upon myself as a normal middle-aged man, who tries to survive in this world and do the best for his family. Suddenly, instead of it being someone on the TV news whose way of life is under threat, it is me, and millions like me, who are in a state of limbo! So, here is the ordinary tale of an ordinary man, who just wants to survive in this world.

I moved to Denmark, together with my family, in 2010. We came for economic reasons, that is to say, to avoid the economic uncertainty after the 2008 financial crisis. By chance, the opportunity arose of a good job with a Danish company that is a world leader in my profession of civil engineering. I came, settled in very well to my new job and found an apartment for us to rent. Then my wife and son joined me and we started the process of integrating and making our home in a new country.

I don't like being called an expatriate. It is a name with 'baggage'. To me, 'expatriate' sounds too much like being a member of an exclave, separated from the society in which it is physically located and hanging on for dear life against some awful doom-laden eventuality, from which we can only be rescued by a Royal Navy gun boat. When I moved to Denmark, I felt like an individual, who, as a citizen of a European Union country, had the right to stand up on his own two feet and take up the offer of a job in another EU country. That was my status, and I was quite happy and, indeed, proud of that.

Over the eight years that I have lived in Denmark, I have found the Danes to be a tolerant, democratic and socially aware society, where both the individual and the community matter. The country has high taxes, but the state social system provides services to its people. Danes work hard and have high standards in business, which is at the heart of why they 'punch above their weight' internationally in some fields, including my own. On the morning after the Referendum, the news of the result left me feeling like someone in the family had died. Bereavement really is the nearest term I can use to describe that feeling. In those first few weeks, there were all sorts of rumours flying around. I have permanent leave to remain in Denmark, but that is based on EU law, so would my status be assured in the future? On the basis of my status, I had bought a house, but would property ownership remain legal for non-EU citizens? These, and others, were real worries. Not least, my son had grown up from 9 to 15 in the Danish state school system. How would he survive in the very different UK education system if we were to be 'sent home'? How could I disrupt his life so profoundly for a second time? Who would ever give me a job back in the UK? Return would also be humiliating.

All of my Danish friends and colleagues, who have shared an opinion, think that the UK is crazy to be leaving the European Union. All I have ever received from them is support, tempered with disbelief at what was and is happening. Their support has been marvellous.

Since summer 2016, I have tried to ignore the press and TV news, because there are very few facts. But the stress of not knowing has been a burden that I have handled with varying success from time to time, and which has left me depressed and feeling isolated.

Tomorrow morning the sun will rise again, as it has done every day for quite some time. A new dawn brings new hope. That at least is something good to hold on to.

A., Denmark

Brexit has made everything more difficult and complicated and stolen so much joy. It's now a permanent preoccupation. I have tried not to let family relationships suffer even though I know close family members in the UK voted leave because of immigration. My French family doesn't seem to understand what difference it makes to my life. In general, they seem to think it's a lot of fuss about nothing, that nothing in my life is going to change. Wrong. My whole outlook has changed and I suffer because of the lack of understanding of my pain.

Anne, France

★★★

I have lived in Norway for 30 years with my wife and 3, now grown up, children. But I grew up in Somerset, and studied and worked in planning in the Midlands and Teesside for some years, before emigrating. Once I could feel and start to understand the fair and inclusive way things work in this social-democratically organized Nordic world, there was no going back for me. Norway sadly said No to joining the EU in 1994, but is, in many ways, at least as much a member as the UK. As a small and peripheral (and rich) country, cooperation with the neighbours is essential for Norway's trade and stability.

In the last 10 years, I have been lucky enough to work in city-to-city international cooperation, spending a lot of time in Brussels and other EU cities and capitals. Besides the work and projects, this has given me a unique insight into how parts of the EU really work from inside, as well as getting behind the first impressions, and generously included as an equal colleague, in every country and city that I have visited. And I have nothing other than respect and admiration for the humble dedication and professionalism of all those whom I have met in public administrations, and in private, through these years.

On 23 June last year, I was in Amsterdam together with an EU-funded network of colleagues from 7 cities and EU countries, (sadly no UK cities). Waking in the night, I tuned in to get the first glimpse of the results – which turned into the nightmare of today. It felt as if the floor collapsed underneath me. Being in Amsterdam on that day felt like home from home. Sharing the loss with team companions, all of them committed to doing their bit in achieving the visions of Europe, I simply cracked up. The tragedy of what had happened that night was just so enormous, and they all understood.

More than a year has passed, and things have gone about as badly as could be imagined. Except that the roles are reversed in my mind. Instead of the UK continuing to do pretty well, despite the wrecking ball, and the EU unravelling, as I had feared might have happen, there are increasingly strong signs that the reverse is playing out. The UK is already hitting some very hard rocks and it will get a lot worse. Meanwhile, the rest of Europe has kept its cool, with its own challenges and agendas, and seems happy to leave the Brexit negotiations to Barnier with a clear mandate. The spectacle of the UK's madness and self-induced suffering is enough to motivate even the most reluctant EU states to keep working at it together.

I still have my UK passport, which gets me easily around Europe for work and holidays. But soon I'll have to decide. Norway does not accept dual nationality, and my UK passport may soon only be eligible for visa applications. Norwegian nationality is definitely an option, though one that is still hard to swallow as it's not of my own choosing.

I have come to understand how every European country has its own unresolvable, agonizing and guilty narratives about what happened in the last century. Families, communities and countries were bitterly divided at the time, forced to decide between supporting totalitarian forces, (Nazi, fascist or communist), or opposing them. Reconciliation has taken generations in many countries, and in the former communist countries is still being worked out. Stories of Nazi collaborators and locally led Jewish deportations are still coming to light in the formerly occupied countries. Other perspectives emerge too, such as when the Mayor of Brno (Czech Republic) recently apologised for his predecessors having forcefully deported tens of thousands of innocent, Czech German speakers from their homes to East Germany in the summer of 1945. Britons were thankfully never forced to make these kinds of choices, that is until 23 June 2016, as if by a haunting echo from the European past that "we" were never a direct part of. As many have said, and all these testimonies confirm, the country has never been less divided since that day.

My workplace was the proud host to the Nobel Peace Prize award to the EU in December 2012. Every EU country was represented by their heads of state or heads of government at the time. Except for Cameron who noticeably sent Clegg.

My children are grown up enough to understand very well what is happening, and don't like what they see. My own feelings of British identity are getting thinner by the day. I count myself lucky to be on the right side of the North Sea, and to have gained such an insight into the unfathomable value of international cooperation in the EU. As a peace project, the EU is unmatched by anything else, and as a project for destruction Brexit is hard to beat in our part of the world.

Peter Austin, Norway

★★★

When I retired after 26 years in commerce in Germany, my Finnish wife and I settled in Finland; no need to claim German citizenship thought I, I am a European!!...? How wrong can you get.

But I had prepared for my retirement by studying theology. I now spend my time as a fully licensed Deacon of the Church of England, with an oath to our Queen. Through the Porvoo Agreement, I am now the Assistant to the Chaplain of the Anglican Church in Finland, Helsinki. I carry out this role by helping the Finnish Lutheran Church here in Vaasa to provide services in English.

We are a very mixed lot, from very many European, Asian and African countries with one common denominator, in addition to Christianity, and that is a workable second language which is English. The community consists mostly of young singles and families with small children living permanently in the area, together with a few Erasmus students.

Who says that we British can't contribute something very positive to the continent? We are now active ambassadors of our country in Europe, so what then are we after Brexit? Frankly, exactly the same. And that is where Brexit is a tragedy. We do contribute and will continue to contribute from our 'mother' culture towards a very positive and wonderful future in Europe. But it would be easier and better if the rest of Britain were behind us.

I could weep when I read what those Brexiteers say about those who like me voted with our feet way over 40 years ago.

Revd. David Oliver, Finland

★★★

A year to go until we leave the EU and I'm still as angry as I was on 24th June 2016. I have never been like this for so long before. It saddens me greatly that we are leaving due to lack of understanding and lack of education about the EU and what it means to the UK. It has split families and friends of long standing and whatever happens it will not get back to how it was before the vote all very sad and unnecessary.

I love my life in France, where I've lived for 19 years, but like any country it isn't perfect, in fact a couple of years ago I had thought of going back to the UK but, because of Brexit, it is the last place I want to go. The pull of family and friends was strong but a few differences of opinion and cross words later I've decided to stay here! There isn't a day that goes by when I don't get wound up about something to do with Brexit which doesn't help the stress levels and I'm meant to be retired and enjoying myself. My husband and I ran a small gîte business here for 12 years before retiring 5 years ago. We now live on our pensions so had to reduce some of our spending, then Brexit hit and we have seen a further 20% – 30% reduction in our income. I am probably better off than some but it is still a big hit and our lifestyle isn't what I had hoped so I am even more depressed as a result! We have a good life here all the same, with French and British friends. The French are amazed and bewildered by Brexit and say it's not logical, then they ask why, I can't answer them.

I'm saddened by all the hurt, worry and anxiety this has caused, but mostly I'm saddened by the lack of understanding/empathy from some friends and family who voted leave in the UK and can't see my problem – "well you decided to move there".

It's the uncertainty I'm having problems with. If we knew for certain where we stood, good or bad, at least we could then deal with it. It's like putting your life on hold until someone else decided what you can do with it. Not getting the vote in the referendum is a case in point, it was the most undemocratic move to date. It shouldn't be like this for any of us who moved to the EU because we could, for a life of our choosing, and now it's being taken away from us or is it, who knows, so, so sad.

Jane Platts, France

★★★

My daughter and her English husband moved to France 15 years ago – his parents have also lived there for 20 years. She now has three children all born there – all bilingual and very happy in France.

As soon as the referendum was proposed, I felt dread – what if the UK voted to leave the EU? Would they have to come back? To leave their life in France would destroy them. I felt deep anger and resentment towards those who would do this to others. That feeling deepened when the results came in. My daughter didn't seem too worried, they had Residency, but I still felt uneasy.

My late husband had wanted us to move to France too, but at that time I had a lot going on in the UK and didn't want to leave. I said I wouldn't mind a second home there, but we couldn't afford it. Then he died and I found myself able to afford a small French house. My daughter said I should move there for family support later on, which seemed sensible. I planned to go in a few years' time, when as she put it, I might need looking after…

Article 50 with its deadline of having to be living in the EU before the UK left in March 2019 meant that if I was going to move to France, I would have to find, buy and furnish a house, and decide what to do with my UK house i.e. sell it or rent it out, in the space of 18 months. I felt resentful at being forced into it before I was ready. All the houses near my daughter were either out of my budget or too rural – unlike some, I didn't want to be in the middle of nowhere in an emergency. I began to panic – what if I couldn't find a house in time? Eventually found a small house – not perfect but it ticked some of my boxes, so I started the buying process. Then the Transition Period was announced, and more letters to politicians imploring them to include citizens' rights along with businesses in the implementation period, to give us all a level playing field – and myself a bit more leeway. Again the EU was supportive, but the UK government resisted as usual, until it eventually caved in under pressure.

But the Citizens' Rights agreement has the caveat that "Nothing is agreed until everything is agreed." So it is not ring-fenced and could fall apart if the UK and the EU do not reach a final deal. Many British people are moving to EU countries regardless. Not least to turn their backs on this narrow-minded, xenophobic little island. But on a very limited budget, reciprocal healthcare and social rights are crucial for me to be able to afford to live in France. So I'm going, but I still feel very uneasy. There are no guarantees for my future. That is not a pleasant feeling when you're 70.

Jacky O'Callaghan, UK

I really don't know where to begin with the impact of the vote in the UK to leave the European Union. Neither do I know any more where I belong. I was able to exercise my right to vote in the referendum, unlike many others who like me, found their life took them off our island. I also exercised my right to free movement just over three and half years ago.

I am in, what I refer to, as my 'third trimester': the one where life experiences, understanding and growth in mental acumen are supposed to make us wiser: but I am not. I do not understand it. I do not understand the abject hatred and xenophobia that I see on social media. I do not understand the misinformation and downright lies being promulgated in the country of my birth. I do not understand how people can vote to make a bad situation so much worse. I do not understand how there can be so much homelessness. I do not understand where food banks came from or why people have to rely on them. I do not understand so much more now than I ever did before.

I left the UK for a job. My children had become independent adults. My mother had passed away. My father and one of my children supported each other through their daily night and day-mares, generated by wars in and outside of the European Continent. I made plans for my own old age. I sold my property in the UK and in 2007, purchased and renovated my home in Bulgaria. I managed to move into it in 2014. I chose Bulgaria for solitude, for peace and quiet, for nature, for a people learning anew about democracy, anti-corruption and how to provide for and care for each other outside of the shackles of communism.

Life was good. I had a plan. I had control of my life and of decisions that affected, and would continue to affect me, for the rest of my life. At least, I thought I had. I won't have completed my five years by the end of March 2019. I may have opportunities to take Bulgarian citizenship, if I ever get fully to grips with the Cyrillic alphabet and language, but why should I now have to? I had and still have European citizenship. A citizenship that does not limit me to living in just one country. A citizenship that enables and facilitates those who don't have degrees to move and work throughout diverse, culturally rich environments in 28 countries, (soon to be 27), if the farce of leaving the European Union proceeds. A citizenship that has enabled oldies like me to retire in a different country in the EU28 if they so wished. What does the future hold now? What control do I have now of my own destiny? Who the hell knows …. I certainly have the least amount of control that I have ever had.

I wrote to my MP in the UK. Nothing of substance in response – a glib "If you want to continue living outside the UK, nothing can stop you and your pension rights remain unaffected." Guess I shall just remain where I am – being treated like a mushroom and "In Limbo Too".

Mary, Bulgaria

★★★

In the extreme case of the hardest of possible Brexits, if bargaining-chip tactics prevail and go awry, I could be forced to close my consulting business in France and leave my 3 French kids and my French girl-friend. This is highly unlikely, but Brexit has already deeply changed who I am.

My identity is deeply affected, as the French would say, it has been "bouleversé", traumatised. I'm a Brit living in Paris. The youngest of my 3 children lives with me half the time, the others have their own flats. I run a French business and have a Parisian girlfriend with young children of her own who cannot leave Paris even if she were welcome in the UK.

I always thought my sense of not truly belonging anywhere was in my head only, not linked to the outside world. Brexit was my wake-up call.

As a Caucasian male, I haven't really experienced discrimination. My grandparents and my father, as Jews in 1930s Austria, went through the worst possible kind. Part of my father's huge pride in his acquired British nationality, I realize now, must have spilled into me. His inex-haustible gratitude must be where I got my blind faith in the underly-ing openness and fairness of Britain and the British people. It was the deepest of trans-generational prides and it was a central part of who I was. It's no longer there and I feel lost; it hurts.

My sense of sadness and foreboding grows with each visit to the UK since the referendum. Whenever I speak to my kids and they answer me in French in public, I get a feeling that we're trespassing and will soon be asked to leave.

15 years ago, my involvement in local politics meant that having French nationality would have been useful. At the time, I was asked

to supply my father's naturalization papers from 1938... I couldn't deal with this level of bureaucracy and I simply gave up as it was a "nice to have" thing not a "must have" at the time. My motivation to plough through the bureaucracy was fine this time round and my new French nationality application was posted nine months after the Brexit referendum.

Feeling British, until June 2016 at least, has made me wear my England rugby shirt on match days, especially against France. I must have defended English cuisine a thousand times to the French. I am a Brit - even though, because of my schooling, I know all the major dates of French history but don't know much about Cromwell.

So, why do I feel so bad about Brexit?

My usually optimistic humanism had me believe that being truly bilingual, i.e. thinking, dreaming in either language, having grown up around the world and being fully multi-cultural, was a privilege which gave me something tangible to contribute to society. When the Prime Minister of Britain said, in the context of Brexit, that citizens of the world are, in fact, citizens of nowhere, I couldn't believe what I was hearing. I felt incredulity and anger. Her hurtful and reactionary statement was about me, yet she had no regard for me, she was just instrumentalising me to address the darker side of her electorate's prejudices.

If the situation degrades with a hard Brexit and even if I could wiggle through regulations to stay in France as an unwelcome migrant, I doubt I would want to. There are many variations on the feeling of not being welcome and, of course, we aren't as nearly badly off as Syrian refugees. But EU citizens have never been part of the cohorts of the unwelcome before in my lifetime. Brexit is a first in so many horrible ways.

I'm 53 and Brexit is for the rest of my life and probably also my children's. So, until the Brexit divorce is irrevocable, I will refuse to accept the dominant narrative that it's only about how and when, no longer if. I will fight Brexit until it happens, then, if we lose, campaign to reverse it.

Ben Schwarz, Paris

★★★

I have been living, working and travelling in Germany/Central Europe for 40 years and am now retired, living near Karlsruhe.

I always identified both as a Brit émigré in Germany and, from the late 90s onwards, as an EU citizen. As with many others, I viewed the increasing negativity in the UK towards the EU, culminating in the referendum in 2016, with concern, and then alarm, once the result was in and the stark reality of Brexit loomed.

My outrage and concern is not least due to potentially having my EU citizenship stolen from me, without having had a say in the process. My experiences probably mirror those of countless other Brits in Europe, so do not want to dwell too much on that.

Early 2017, my wife and I went on a guided tour around the France-Germany border area near Karlsruhe – an area that has seen many wars over the past two centuries, as evidenced by the countless war cemeteries dotted around. We were taken to the small town of St. Germanshof near Wissembourg, which, in 1950, was the setting of a symbolic, peaceful "storming" of the sleepy border post by students, (Bund der Europäischen Jugend), from across Europe, (including from the UK), when they broke down the barrier and crossed the border without passports.

And this was 7 years before the Treaty of Rome was signed, signifying the beginning of the European project.

This image of a post-war generation of young people protesting for a united, borderless Europe to enable its citizens to live in peace and prosperity continues to bring a lump to my throat, particularly when considering how much risk they took upon themselves at the time.

A monument, consisting of 12 columns arranged in a circle, symbolising the EU flag, has been erected at the site to commemorate this event – an ideal place for quiet reflection on the origins and real meaning of the EU.

Immediately after this visit, I processed my citizenship application, and since January 2018 am a proud citizen of Germany. Just as important, though, is the assurance that my EU citizenship can no longer be taken away from me.

My learning from this is that the freedoms we enjoy here in the EU need to be constantly fought for, and not taken for granted. Here we are, 70 years after the end of WW2 and it seems that we are in danger of repeating the mistakes of the past.

Peter Ellis, Germany

★★★

I'm English, but I was born in Holland and lived there for 18 years. Holland feels like home to me, but I've also lived 12 years in Spain, where my daughter, whose mother is Spanish, was born and continues to live. At the time of the EU referendum I was actually living back in the UK because my parents are elderly and my mum has Alzheimer's, they moved back on retirement 20 years ago.

The last few years I've been living a sort of double life between the UK and Spain and I need to continue to do so. How can I choose between helping elderly, ill parents and my daughter? I have to be able to move freely between the two countries, I don't have a choice, but the idea that I might not be able to return 'back home' to Holland one day, makes me genuinely depressed. I could have applied for a Dutch passport at 18 but that option is no longer available to me. Basically I couldn't be more European if I tried; for me it's not a political stance or choice, it's just a fact.

David S., Spain & UK

I was in America the night of the referendum, and because of the time difference I could watch all the results coming in. I couldn't believe what I was seeing! When I came down to breakfast in the hotel the next morning my Belgian colleagues jokingly told me to go and sit on a different table.

I've lived in Belgium with my family since 1996. 2 of my 3 children were born there: all of them have been at school in French since kindergarten and are bilingual. The immediate reaction of the whole family was to request Belgian nationality as a way of protecting our European rights. For the children this is mostly about work: with their international outlook they expect to live and work in Europe and didn't want to be limited. My wife is a civil servant, working for the Belgian government. Her job was only opened to EU citizens, as opposed to Belgians, a couple of years ago. How would Brexit affect her position?

My youngest son has two passions: rugby and planes. He's had trials for the Belgian national junior rugby team, and is a member of the

Belgian Air Cadets: both of these are only open to EU citizens. I bet no one who voted Leave was voting to stop a young British lad from following his dreams, but that's a sad outcome of the referendum.

My older kids got Belgian nationality easily, and we're lucky that Belgium allows dual nationality. They're both at university in Britain. Oddly the oldest was prevented from applying for certain jobs in UK defence industries as you can't apply if you hold dual nationality, but his Belgian nationality is more important. My youngest will be applying for university in a couple of years: will he be treated as an EU student, (same fees as UK student), or as an international student, with potentially much higher fees? We're looking into other universities in Europe even though we all prefer the UK style of teaching.

It took 3 appeals for my wife to get her Belgian nationality, due to silly bureaucracy, but she has it now so feels protected.

I delayed submitting my request: I think I believed deep down that somehow Brexit wouldn't happen, but in March 2018 I decided I couldn't wait any longer so I applied. I feel betrayed and let down by the UK government – they don't seem to understand the many issues facing UK nationals in EU, or don't seem to care. In Belgium the local government people have been very friendly and helpful with all our applications. But it's been expensive and bureaucratic, and could easily have been avoided. And we're lucky: we can have dual nationality. It would have been a much more difficult decision if we'd had to give up our British nationality.

I feel like the family is all protected now, but Brexit is a constant source of stress to us. It's the first topic of conversation amongst people here. On a skiing holiday recently whenever I heard an English voice my first thought was "which way did you vote?" I hate it, and I wish some politicians would have the guts to stand up and say what a damaging issue this is for Britain.

John, Belgium

★★★

This morning I was granted the decision that confirms that I and my two year old son will be given Austrian citizenship subject to renouncing our British citizenship, as double citizenship is not allowed when naturalising as an Austrian citizen.

My case officer has not been particularly competent – I have by and large outwitted her by having observed my Russian wife's procedure with her for her naturalisation (running since 2014). Of course Britons naturalising is a new thing, but for both the case officer and her supervisor to claim that they are unaware of minors not being able to renounce their citizenships is something I find hard to believe. All being well now, I think that my choice will also help others in my position, as there are more people who will go through this. I will be issued the Bescheid der Zusicherung der Verleihung der österreichischen Staatsbürgerschaft as soon as two documents are submitted.

Once we have proved that we have instigated our renouncing of British citizenship, my son and I will have our citizenship ceremony. He is only 2 so I've got him a little Austrian flag to wave around the house.

We are of course sad and angry that we are having to renounce our British citizenship, but also happy to see the light at the end of the tunnel of bureaucracy, with our Russian/British family uniting as an Austrian one.

Mike Bailey, Austria

★★★

My name is Kathy, I am married to a French woman, (Mellie), and have been resident in France since 1993. Most of my friends, acquaintances and extended family have always been hostile towards Europe. If it came up in conversation they'd go "Aach! The EU!!" or "Europe! What a basket case!" so I would avoid mentioning the EU, and Europeans come to that, seeing as individual nationalities also got that treatment. I regret lacking the pluck to never have argued back, but would it have made a difference? I'm fortunate that Mum, my brother and I share the same strong pro-Europe sentiments, to have been divided over this – with them – would have been a tragedy. The rest don't matter, they can look after themselves.

So the referendum result didn't surprise me but was nevertheless devastating. I tried not to let it get me down but as the months passed it increasingly dominated my thoughts. As uncertainty increased, I applied for French Nationality by naturalisation.

I've previously made two moves to become French but they laughed at me, with more or less the following rejoinders each time: "But why bother? You're European! Why clog up the immigration system?? You don't need to do this when thousands who aren't from the EU need this more than you? What a waste of money!! You already have so many rights! Don't you realise how lucky you are?…"

I then said I was concerned about the changing anti-EU atmosphere in the UK. Aha, I was really shot down then. Mellie said that NO ONE would be THAT stupid in the UK to want to leave the EU, and she said I was being very silly. I gave up the process which was expensive enough without having it equated to a paranoid vanity project. Following the referendum Mellie and the handful of people who discouraged me apologized most humbly. I confess that when we moved here I had an underlying mind-set that we English were better. We knew how to do things – anything better than the French!

Certainly better than other Europeans! This jingoism wasn't something constantly in my head, far from it, but from the outset it skewed any perception I had of what went on in Europe. I've since taken back that stupid bigoted reasoning.

I was a teen in the 1970s when the cultural atmosphere was frankly 'colourful'. Comedies such as Fawlty Towers, and 'Allo 'Allo were all too easily taken at a puerile level that allowed the belittling and distancing of foreigners. I took this snickering attitude with me to France, and I really don't know how patient Mellie put up with some of my assertions. But as the years passed my arrogant ignorance faded as I got to know more about Europe, and got to know more Europeans as well as more French people.

My bigotry decreased also because my spoken and written French kept improving.

Then there is the increasing interest and pride in what other people, (other than Brits), do and think, and when seeing achievements from other European nations that at least equal if not excel those from the UK, I can enjoy being impressed and proud, no longer taking foreign excellence as a disturbance to my notion of Englishness.

Now I get sad when I think of England. I love the countryside and the pretty brick villages of Vale of White Horse, (where I'm from), the Chilterns, the Downs, Oxford. I love much of British culture, films, literature and comedy… But the thought of those things that used to give me pleasure – even the countryside – are now tainted.

When I visit Mum in Oxfordshire I drive, in a car with left-hand drive and French plates. Since the referendum noticed a change from drivers and pedestrians. I now get the odd broad smile which I love but I've also received some hard aggressive glares and to date, two pairs of fists have been shaken at me.

On the contrary I haven't heard any anti-English hostility from the French I know or meet, I've read no nasty and childish "blame British *forrinners* go home" crap from the French press, radio or TV, and know of no menacing announcements from the French State. Personally I have received friendly and sympathetic enquiries and condolences. A guy at a party asked me about Brexit, he was pro the idea, (but only for Britain to do it), but never said that I or Brits should go home or get French nationality or anything like that.

No one in power or authority in the UK is condemning the nebulous, unorganised but very real passive-aggressive social climate, as expressed by some of the press and public, where many Europeans are being bullied and intimidated, an atmosphere that slyly nudges them to leave. It's the Hostile Environment. I get very angry about this, the 3 million are being treated in a disgraceful way, they are being roundly ignored by most everyone in Government/Parliament except for the issuing of hollow platitudes. Thankfully campaign groups like In Limbo exist to give them a voice and make their plight known.

While the atmosphere has become difficult in the UK, while I no longer take much pleasure in being English, I count myself fortunate. This energy and solidarity of the Remain Fellowship has been a tremendous joy and succour to me, I feel equally strongly that this will be a strong force for good.

Kathy, France

★★★

It's half term, and we're back over in the UK to see family.

My father-in-law still lives in a small (former) mining town. He's always worked hard – so hard he had to retire early because he was physically worn out. Consequently, he has little time for people who expect life to be handed to them on a plate. He never had much chance at a decent education, but he's a clever and generous man with a unique sense of humour.

He approves of us moving abroad, because it's for work.

He walks to the newsagents every day to buy a copy of the Daily Express. Before the referendum, I was able to have a reasonable conversation with him about leave or remain, and I'd like to think he was undecided in the run-up. Now, however, nearly 18 months later, his language on the subject has changed significantly.

This week, the main story in the Express is about the foreign aid budget. Yes, you guessed it – don't spend it on foreigners! It's a very sustained attack – the front-page headline and article is backed up with a leader column and more articles by household names like Jacob Rees-Mogg and Nigel Farage. 3 days in a row. The message is hammered in again, and again, and again.

This isn't news. It's manipulation. And with my father-in-law, it works. He's certainly not a bad person by any stretch of the imagination. He is, however, our one and only Brexiteer in the family. If his health worsens, it's not impossible that he might want to move in with us. We'd have him anytime – despite his somewhat dubious political perspective, he's still great company and a lovely man and we all love him dearly.

But we don't know if that will be possible post Brexit – we don't know if he'd be able to move to Belgium on his state pension, and we don't know what would happen to the healthcare tab.

But what upsets me most of all is that his great grandchildren, when they eventually arrive, will not have the same rights to live and work in Britain as his children and grandchildren. Everything he has taken for granted, they will not have. I just can't explain that to him.

He doesn't know it, he doesn't understand it, but he's in limbo too.

J. Thomas, Belgium

★★★

Hello from Germany.

My partner and I came here in September 2015 for her work, initially a six-month trainee placement. This was extended several times; now it's two and half years later and we are still here.

After the vote in June 2016, I was extremely upset but I thought maybe it's possible to make it work. Surely the people in charge had a plan.

It became clear very quickly that no-one had a plan. Most likely that no-one on either side really thought that the public would vote leave and therefore no preparation had been done. Since then the news has just got worse, the nonsense and fantasy more bizarre every single day.

It makes me think I was naive; clearly the undercurrent of mistrust, xenophobia and outright hatred had always been part of the country I grew up in, and Brexit had merely given it oxygen. It was like everyone from your slightly racist Gran to the really crazy Britain First crew had been given permission to speak their minds for the first time in 30 odd years. The country voted out, so surely everyone else must think like me? In the same way, as the constant drip drip drip of anti-science, anti-facts, anti-'the other' news from the mainstream, (predominantly right-wing), press in the UK has ruined any chance of the EU ever receiving a fair hearing; this constant drip drip drip of hate, spin and ill-informed drivel is making me doubt that I could ever go back. It's also hard to imagine how the country can go back;

it will be a long time before the country can be taken seriously again. To think that London 2012 celebrated everything great about the UK, and seemingly brought everyone together. How can it have gone so wrong so quickly?

Contrary to popular belief, the immigration rules in Germany are quite strict. My language skills have never been that great and anyway there isn't time to accrue the necessary time lived here before all this shit implodes, (or explodes?)

I now feel isolated and alone. Outside of our apartment and a couple of very supportive online groups it's become pretty much impossible to discuss these feelings. Even our British friends here rarely bring up the subject, although I suspect many of them are also feeling lost.

What is the end game for those steering the country towards the cliff edge for some kind of impromptu mass suicide? Empire 2.0 based on imaginary British exceptionalism? What kind of crazy world pits the old, some uneducated racists and a few wealthy elites against the best interests of the country? I have no idea. The one thing I am sure about is that the biggest issues facing humanity, climate change, mass migration, the rise of authoritarianism can only be solved with the kind of cooperation born out of the ashes of WWII and fostered by what is now the EU.

Now I'm going to ride my bicycle in the woods. It's literally the only thing that makes sense anymore.

Ollie, Germany

★★★

Heartbreak of British European.

Growing up in Belgium, with British parents who left Thatcherite UK, I was, at first, surprised everyone didn't speak English and sometimes felt an outsider. I integrated but was "the English girl", I longed to return to the UK, and went back to university and experienced the euphoria of Blair's win – the future looked bright. After missing the UK for so long, the ignorance of my peers about Europe was shocking and my arguments about the EU meant "I couldn't be British, I wasn't patriotic enough".

I met my Swedish husband there, in the UK, and married in 1999, then mum was diagnosed with cancer and died. We took charge of my two brothers, (8 & 14), as dad travelled for work, (we were in Worcester), and we decided to move closer to my sister in Belgium, with our 1-year-old and my brothers. We had two more children there and, after 5 years, moved to Sweden to experience the culture and live in the countryside. Four years on Gotland, two more children and I was offered the opportunity to teach in Kenya and moved with 5 children to Gilgil. Although incredible it was not home – unlike Germany, Belgium, France... basically the EU. Our time there was cut short as dad, (in the UK), got terminal cancer. We got back on 11 November and dad passed on 14th. He was cared for by wonderful NHS staff. We settled in Nottingham and bought a house, the kids went to good schools. One more child arrived and we joked he would never live abroad as we couldn't imagine leaving again. We watched Question Time as they trotted out Farage ad nauseam and laughed at him. Then Cameron won the election based on giving referendum and fear-mongering about SNP-Labour. We couldn't conceive Britain would vote leave. I was the only one with a vote and campaigned, with our "I'm In" t-shirts; my 7-year-old and I faced verbal abuse and she was very shaken. I attended Question-time with Michael Gove and asked about the impact on my service company, he made his stock German car response. Then Jo Cox was murdered. After that I felt very apprehensive. I knew then, a leave vote meant leaving the UK. I stayed up for the results and the tears came, I was glued to my settee. I didn't want to go out and see the Leave posters, I took down the Stronger In and EU flag out of fear, I watched as the leave campaign reneged, no 350 million for the NHS, etc. as sterling plummeted, the government disappeared and the lack of understanding became clear. I cannot express the grief, how my heart broke, how I felt my country rejected my values, my family, tolerant openness, I was forced to choose between being a European or British citizen. Before I was proud to be a British European now it was either or and – no contest – European wins. The grief is that I will never again be proud to be British. We held a mini-referendum: Ireland, Spain, France, Germany, Sweden or Belgium, no question of the UK. In July 2016, we put the house on the market, by October our life in the UK was history, and we were in our new home. Of the eight of us, only I risk losing my European citizenship. In four years, I will apply to become Belgian.

The foolishness and incompetence of the British government is limitless with little idea of the complexities of 40 years of interlinked legislation, or even parliamentary sovereignty and constitutional law. A blind misunderstanding that the European Project is solely about trade – it is much more. My grandfathers fought in WWII, my grandmother lived with us until she died and lived through two wars, lost her father in the trenches, Nana's stories of war and loss and the importance of peace in Europe will stay with me forever.

We moved full circle, my parents left for Belgium in the 1980s because of a Tory woman Prime Minister and we did the same over thirty years later. Our boy who wouldn't live abroad has taken to Flemish nursery like a duck to water, we will not look back.

Greta Holmer, Belgium

★★★

A year to the day since Article 50 was triggered. A year to the day until Brexit happens. Sitting in limbo in my Provençal studio, I'm struggling to express my thoughts. A painter and linguist, my creativity and my words have been sucked almost dry by Brexit. Some days I feel broken.

Where did my European journey start? What has made me feel so passionately about remaining a European citizen that Brexit has driven me from the UK? After all I'm English by birth. Why is Britain no longer my home?

When I was nearly five my father moved us to France, to Paris, my mother, my younger sister and myself, setting my life on its nomadic course and enriching me immensely. When we returned to the UK, three French schools and five years later, I was bilingual and had formed an enduring attachment to France.

It was a shock to land in a small village school in Lancashire, where my sister and I were called 'the Frenchies' by our new classmates. But I adapted – children are resilient – and went on to enjoy European Studies at a British university before setting off overseas again, first working back in France and later further afield, in Egypt. There I experienced a fascinating and very different culture which confirmed my roots: Europe had already shaped my thoughts and outlook more than I'd realised.

Fast forward a couple of decades spent working mainly in the UK, where I met my husband, a proud Welshman with a passion for mountains and caves – he would spend hours exploring underground while I preferred to paint the landscape above. In 2007, we set off on an adventure: running painting holidays at our Provençal bed and breakfast – living the dream half way up a mountainside overlooking lavender fields, hilltop villages and with our very own olive trees. In reality a lot of hard work – and an amazing experience.

Eventually we made a big decision: to return to the UK, to run painting courses there and take groups of painters to Provence twice a year. Late in 2015 we bought a house, moved to Somerset and unpacked every single box, believing we'd be there for the duration.

Just seven months later, the UK held a referendum. I was in shock at the result. I went to bed in the early hours of 24 June with a sinking feeling, having seen the results come in first from Sunderland – Leave. After a few hours' sleep the worst news was confirmed. At seven twenty – the time is ingrained in my mind – I was posting on Facebook my reaction: "What has the UK done? Collective f★★★★★★g madness!"

The day before the referendum was the last day my world felt normal. We'd spent it together, celebrating our twentieth wedding anniversary with an exquisite meal at a very special gastropub on the edge of Dartmoor, driving home through wild and beautiful scenery. That's the last day I remember being truly carefree. Ever since, there's been a feeling of dread in my mind. Sometimes it's at the back of my mind, but mostly it's at the forefront, colouring everything. There's a knot of anguish in my guts. I wake up on many nights at four in the morning; I have nightmares and health issues, mainly related to Brexit stress.
I tried to adapt. But the referendum result did something to me. I lost all motivation to put down roots in a country that no longer seemed like home. I felt alien, living in the middle of Leave country, with Leave signs polluting the fields even months after the campaign was over. How was I to feel at home among people holding such fundamentally different world views?

Slowly I began campaigning and it's now part of my daily life. The fight to stop Brexit is exhausting and demoralising. Luckily my family is intact. But I've lost friends of many years' standing over irreconcilable differences in values.Craig

People ask why Brexit matters so much to me. They don't understand that I feel I'm losing a precious part of my identity as my EU citizenship is ripped away from me against my will. For no good reason: in twenty one months, no one has been able to give me a justifiable reason to Brexit. When I dig down, it always comes down to two vile things: racism and xenophobia. Fear of 'the other'.

Some understand better when I explain how the practical implications of Brexit affect me: the pension contributions I paid into the French state system over the years are subject to whatever final Brexit deal is agreed. I've become a bargaining tool for the UK government. Financial uncertainty threatens my future retirement plans. A Leave voting 'friend' of over twenty years' standing told me that it was my own stupid fault for working in another country. That hurt. As an EU citizen I was perfectly entitled to and, I believed, protected in doing so. Now that trust is betrayed by a government that has a duty, I naively thought, to look after its citizens. Our plan to run painting courses across two countries was put on hold: no one could tell us how that business would work after Brexit.

Finally, after months of agonising and endless discussions, I left the country. That's how big my protest is. In October 2017 we moved back to the small Provençal market town we'd stupidly left less than two years earlier. I feel I've come home. I'm thankful my husband understood my heartbreak and distress sufficiently to share with me a very different future to the one we envisaged.

Wendy Coleby Watkins, France

★★★

'Why do you hate us?' I lost count of how many times I'd been asked that question at work or how many times I've ended up in tears of frustration and hurt at home because I couldn't give my students or work colleagues an answer because I was wondering the same thing myself... That was a year ago, the question has changed but the feelings of betrayal and despair, both theirs and mine, remain.

Today the questions revolve around what's happening with Brexit, hasn't it been stopped already and if I 'know any suppliers in the Republic of Ireland as the company bosses have decided that they'd rather spend a little more on transport costs to get a comparable quality product than deal with British firms regardless of whether Brexit takes place or not?'. Strangely these questions hurt more than the random taunts of 'When are you going?' from the local ONR supporter because they're usually followed by the questioner trying to reassure me by saying I'll be OK because I'm English and not an immigrant... which turns to shocked looks when I point out that being English means I must be an immigrant and so have no idea whether I will be able to stay, let alone whether the rights I've grown up with, lived with and taken advantage off will be stolen from me and millions of others like me.

Lynn T., Poland

★★★

My sister and I are 50/50 English and Italian, she was born in Italy in the late 40s, I was born in London in the early 60s. We've never been close due to the age gap which I think defined our attitudes towards the EU and Europe. My sister and her partner are both Daily Mail readers and they both voted Leave.

I've never felt British/English or Italian, I only used "British" to tick a box – what I do feel is European. I tried for an Italian passport many years ago, I was talked out of it by a member of Consulate staff who said "You won't need it, with the burgundy passport, you get the same rights and freedoms as everyone else in the EU". I've since found that I don't qualify for one anyhow.

In May 2015 I took early retirement and in August 2015 we relocated to my new East European EU country. I settled in quickly, without any issues, (I've visited the city many times before), getting Residency was quite easy, bought a car and property but I'm having a slow time learning the language.

I'm starting the process to apply for citizenship of my adopted country in order to retain my EU rights, and jump through the administrative hoops that will come my way. My Fiancée and I will be getting married in June, and we have about 30 friends and family coming from the UK. I've kept quiet about my opinions and our circumstances at the moment so as not to cause any major upset prior to the wedding, and I'm going ask guests not to talk about BREXIT while they're here. I suspect most of them voted Leave, so if we're going to fall out, it's best done after the wedding. I consider my friends to be intelligent and mature enough to accept different points of view but one never knows, especially when alcohol is involved. The friendship dynamic may change after the wedding, once they're aware of my views.

No one knows about my intention of applying for dual nationality yet, and I don't seem to have that uncertainty, (yet?), that others in the same position have. Perhaps that's misplaced, maybe I'll be kicked out of the country I call home and be told to go live in a country that, only after 2.5 years, already feels like a foreign country.

It pains me to see what's happened in the UK since the Referendum was announced, not just for Brits but everyone in and out of the UK. I still don't understand how Leavers couldn't see the damage it would do, cannot see the damage it is has already done, and the damage that it is doing now. And the damage it will continue to do for years to come to the people in the UK and the UK economy.

Anonymous, Romania

★★★

I'm 27 years old and my partner is 30, both born European citizens who used the equivalent rights throughout our entire lives so far – casual holidays across Europe since we can remember. I studied German at university with an Erasmus year in Berlin, and it was always in our plans to move to Germany at some point.

Up until the vote, we'd both lived in London for around 8 years and were slowly getting tired of the pace there and considering a move over to Berlin, but thinking we could plan nicely and that we'd have time to sort out the logistics.

However immediately after the, for us shocking, vote we were forced to immediately start job-hunting and felt that we needed to get here asap to lay down roots for whatever came next. We made it over here just 3 months later in October 2016.

Straight after the vote the bile that came from my side of the family was terrible. I'd known that my political opinions were always more liberal than everyone else's, but suddenly because they'd 'won' they felt it was appropriate to push their opinions and downright bully us for being upset about the life-changing result. For example:

One of my stepbrother's ideas of gloating was to message me the morning after the vote with a screenshot of Ryanair flights to Germany and a comment that we should start packing our bags... We aren't close and this wasn't meant as a joke.

My father, who ironically owns property in Spain, decided to try and lecture us on how it was worth the immediate pain because long-term Britain would be more 'in control'. At one point the arguments became so much that we had to take a 3 month break from talking.

My grandad still sends me an email every few days with a rant about how Britain should walk away from the negotiating table and the 'bullies of Europe', always paired with some pretty vile racist comments.

To add to the stress of it all, after 7 years together we're now looking to get married asap this year.

Given that my other half is freelance, we're not sure what his visa status could be if negotiations did fail and everything that's been promised so far is never signed into law. So instead of slowly saving for and planning the wedding of our dreams, we're aware that we have a deadline and are having to see what we can financially and physically achieve this summer.

Also, unfortunately, because of Brexit we're having to get married here in Germany, despite the majority of friends and family being back in the UK. To get married in England you have to register as a resident and we're afraid to de-register in Germany and lose the time we've already accrued here for any future citizenship applications.

This has then led to even more cannon fodder for the family to attack with and strained our already damaged relationship.

I just don't know how I can reconcile any of their behaviour with the idea of a 'loving family'....

Despite all of that, we're so happy we made the move when we did. We're building a beautiful life here; appreciating the freedoms of the

EU whilst we can and telling everyone proudly that when the vote went the wrong way, we voted again with our feet.

Rebecca, Germany

★★★

Thrust into limbo, EU citizenship is something any of us born after 1991 take for granted. It is not just a symbol of belonging. It is its essence. European integration is founded on people. The indignation felt at the erection of the Berlin wall is felt once more at the scandalous attempt to divide families yet again. Invisible smart borders, as a 'solution' to the Irish border, is nothing more than a recipe for tripe, treating people as if they were barcodes. And yet the threat of Brexit has divided our family: Brexit is a source of anger and resignation. Anger among those who have experienced the joys of having friends, families and children across the EU, living and working in 'Europe'. Resignation among in-laws who deface our EU stickers, scorn our EU marches and clam up if Brexit is mentioned: they, conveniently, 'don't do politics'. But they do fear politics. Family gatherings split as husbands and wives squabble over not inviting relatives who do do politics. Adult children who, rather than see their own children sink in the British Brexit bog, are emigrating; or staying, in limbo, elsewhere in the EU. And us, the generation that helped build the programmes to facilitate cross border life, dumping our British nationality – if we can – in shame.

The mere threat of Brexit has wrecked our lives, created anxiety over our own children living elsewhere in the EU, their homes, the resurgence of bureaucratic squandering of time to get driving licences recognised, cross borders, transfer money, goods, medicines. The deep sorrow the threat of Brexit engenders does not quell the moral repugnance that makes us fight it not just for our own sakes, but for the sake of younger people everywhere in Europe. If Brexit happens it will affect us all: politicians who allow it will have destroyed what it was that once attracted so many to come here. That sense of shame and betrayal is compounded by a loss of hope that now propels many to despair of Britain and assert their Europeanness.

What would our parents and grandparents have made of all this? The blonde teenager stepping off the plane bringing the first 'aliens' to Britain after the war, her excitement at coming to England to marry and 'for a better life'? Our shock at seeing her, our mother, speak impeccable English on a 1946 BBC Newsreel, echoing the sentiment of so many more recent arrivals in England from Europe.

Working for the British Occupying forces as a translator in Berlin, my mother was determined to be as British as she could. Her British fiancé had defied the rules on fraternizing with the enemy and brought her to a country that was ridden with xenophobia. To shield her children from the spite of her new London neighbours, she chose never to speak German. When her younger sister visited, she made her dress like the English. Lots of lipstick. No German, and do voluntary work in hospitals with the Red Cross. This tenacious woman took on the insulting border guards at Dover who turned her sister back for trying to visit England twice in 18 months in the 1950s. She would not have stood by and allowed EU citizenship to be stripped from her children and grandchildren. Nor shall we.

Juliet Lodge, UK

PART II

"We have been deserted, we have been left to paddle without knowing where we are paddling to."

I'm a British citizen and retired psychotherapist, living in Italy.

Before I came to live here I worked in East London. In the year of the 2012 Olympics, I was never so proud of my country, people from around the world welcoming the world! Showing the way to live together.

I would never have believed that in 4 short years all that could change. We moved here to spend our retirement in the beautiful hills of the Sybilline national park later that year, bought a home and found a community which accepted us into their huge hearts.

Until the referendum I considered myself an expat, but in 2016 something happened to my beloved homeland. It was split asunder, now taken over by those who oppose everything I value about it, and who despise my fellow Europeans living there. It truly does break my heart to see this happening.

The week after the referendum, I visited my mother in Clacton. Outside a Polish supermarket I witnessed a shocking event. A large man, baseball bat in hand, stood outside the door. Saying nothing but clearly scaring anyone wanting to enter. When I tried to go into the shop I was called bitch, traitor to my people, and many other names. I'm old enough to deal with this, but why should other people decide what are my country's values? I no longer consider myself a British expat. I am in exile from a country I no longer recognise, to which I cannot return because it no longer exists and which rejects me because of my choices.

In August, and October of that year my community here in Italy was devastated by earthquakes. My home and everything in it was reduced to rubble. But the people here are inspirational. They have faith their community will be reborn, and I chose to take my chances with earthquakes, in a land where buildings are broken but the soul is strong, rather than return to a land where the buildings stand but the soul is broken.

Denise, Italy

★★★

I'm a 58-year-old ex-rugby playing, former Merchant Navy seaman who worked in the oil and gas industry for about 37 years, in various countries. I consider myself quite thick-skinned, independent and capable of managing most situations. I've been on fully loaded LNG carrying ships when they have had fires on board. I have managed emergencies as an Offshore Installation Manager and onshore Production Manager. I think that I've generally trodden my own path and, most of the time, done my bit to provide for a secure future for family and self. My wife and I have always lived well within our means so that we could save for our future; that gave us both a sense of control.

Last week, my wife decided to come home earlier than scheduled to the house in France that we bought about 12 years ago and have invested in as our planned home. I've lived here for almost three years and the plan was that my wife would join me here either this year or next. We've been planning this 'coming together' after about 15 years of one or the other of us working away from previous homes. My wife still lives and works in the UK but came home earlier than scheduled because she was a bit worried about me.

Anyway, it happened like this. My wife called me on Tuesday to say: "Surprise, you'll have to pick me up at Angouleme station tomorrow because I'm arriving then and not next Sunday". Naturally, I was delighted that she was coming home early and duly picked her up on Wednesday. As I'd only been given about 18 hours notice I didn't have time to do all of my pre-wife-arrival housework and felt guilty about it. So, on Thursday morning I set up the ironing board and set to reducing the pile of accumulated cotton and linen while my wife did some remote-working at her desk here. After about one and a half hours, my wife came down for a mid-morning cuppa and chatted to me as the kettle was boiling. She said I'd seem a bit subdued over FaceTime lately and asked if everything was OK. That's when I started to cry inconsolably – with little spurts of steam being generated as my tears got trapped between cloth and iron. I told my wife that I felt as though everything we had carefully saved for was being taken from us and that I had absolutely no control over whether we would be able live as we had planned. I sobbed that there was no certainty over what Brexit would mean for us and that I felt useless and powerless to do anything about it. She knew then why I had seemed a little subdued.

So, there it is. Brexit has created in me emotions that I have never experienced before. I am fortunate not yet to have lost a parent, sibling, child or other close family member but I really do think that I feel bereaved – something is being taken from me and I can't prevent it and have no idea how I can ameliorate its effects because no-one can tell me with certainty what they will be. This really does feel worse to me than being on board an LNG tanker with a fire on board or an off-shore installation with 170 people I'm responsible for and which has a gas leak. I know why it feels worse, because I have no sense of control and don't trust the people who are telling me they will look after us.

Paul, France

★★★

June 23rd, 2016 changed my life. I'm a Brit living in Spain. I've been living in Valencia, Spain, for 8 years with my partner and my two kids. In order for you all to understand my predicament, I need to revert back to my childhood. I grew up in the South of England, in a small village outside of Bath, called Midsomer Norton. My parents were working class. Education, university and travel was always something that 'other people' did. Not us. Anyone who was not white, British or from the UK was treated with suspicion. They weren't as worthy as us, apparently.

But I broke the mould. At the age of 18 I booked a one-way flight to Greece. I never felt comfortable with the life that appeared to be mapped out for me. I was supposed to leave school, go out to work, get married and bring my children up in the 'hub' that was my existence. For some reason, I wanted more. So, I left all that I knew at the age of 18 and travelled. I spent 3 years living in different countries, meeting new people, picking up snippets of different languages, embracing new cultures and realising that the life I had left behind was not for me. I eventually returned to the UK and then put myself through university. I took the grants, the loans, the financial support available in those days. I wanted to learn. I wanted to broaden my horizons. I didn't want to be like my family, see different coloured skin as a threat, have a sense of superiority simply because I was born in the UK. And so, I educated myself. I met partners, had two children, worked, and longed for the day that I could introduce my own children to the wider world and broaden their horizons too.

Eventually I got to a position that I could do that 8 years ago, and I moved to Spain full time. I put both the kids in public schools. They couldn't speak a word of Spanish, but they managed. We all did. We carved a life out for ourselves. We embraced the language, the culture, the traditions. We made new friends. We became an integral part of our community. We were happy. Our lives were enriched. It felt like I had finally found the place I was meant to be. The place I was supposed to bring my children up in, the life I was supposed to give them.

Now we reach 23rd June 2016. The referendum. The time I finally had to face exactly how much of a black sheep I am to my family, realise how different I am from them all, and face the reality that the life I have strived so hard for may now be in jeopardy. My entire family voted leave. Every single one of them. From my parents, to my sister, to my aunties and uncles and to my cousins. There was no consideration for me, or my kids. There was no consideration for the 3 million EU nationals living in the UK. There was no thought for how this would affect Brits living abroad. There was no consideration for anyone else's lives accept their own interpretations of who was worthy to be in the UK, who had the right colour skin and who they considered should be allowed to remain there. It really was that black and white to them. There was no grey area worthy of consideration.

And now we are here. I've lost my family. I've lost the security I felt for 8 years as a Brit in Spain. Can I stay here in Spain, in the place I call home? Brexit has broken society as we know it. My story is not unique. Hundreds of others will tell you the same. We have become a divided nation. We have lost family and lost friends as we realise how different our perspectives are, realise how differently many of us view society and we have been forced to accept that there are some people we love who are simply xenophobic, racist or just downright gullible.

I don't have an answer. I don't know how we repair such intense damage to families, friendship or society. All I do know is that Brexit has turned my life upside down, made my future uncertain and made me look at the people I once loved in such a dark light I see no way back to how we all once were. Brexit has changed my life. And not for the better.

Gemma Middleton, Spain

★★★

As all the post-referendum Brexit rhetoric kicked in, I had an overwhelming feeling of loss and sadness – it was like a death. It was the death of something that I treasured, cared for and thought about constantly: my country, its people and its future.

As the battle-lines have been drawn and then hardened, the situation has forced me to consider taking the nationality of the country which I live in – Germany. Whilst I love where I live, very fond of the inhabitants and really value being in central Europe, I don't feel at all German. I feel totally British. I don't even want to have dual citizenship – but I may have to. Brexit has killed my unquestioning faith in my country. That's why I feel bereaved.

Rupert March, Germany

★★★

I am British and I live in the Netherlands, in one of the provinces that is actually called Holland.

My grandfather, during WWII was posted in Nijmegen, bordering Germany, in the Eastern province of Gelderland. He witnessed the 'hunger winter' when many Dutch people died through starvation, plain and simple, no 'gas chambers'. He did not come home until well into 1946, maybe early 1947. He would not really talk about it, partly because he had been told not to 'under orders', and partly because I think it was too painful for him; he never went 'abroad' again, even for a holiday. I do not know how my grandfather felt about the EEC, (and he died before the formation of the EU proper), but I think I can say with confidence that he would not have liked the UK being ripped asunder from a European Union that has seen 70 years of peace and 60 years of unity.

I have spent more of my adult life in The Netherlands than in Britain. Besides the fact that I have no money, property or close family still alive and resident in the UK, I do not feel that I would 'fit into' British society anymore. So I am truly 'in limbo'; I may be left with nowhere to call home and nowhere to go to.

At this point in time, I am living on Dutch state benefits. It was not my intention to do so and I hope that it will not continue; I have so much to offer in the workplace. As an EU citizen, of long-standing residence, I am entitled to benefits. However, when I am no longer an EU citizen, it is not outside the realms of possibility that I may be asked to leave the country that has become my home. It is standard procedure that for anyone who is not a Dutch citizen that, on applying for full 'social security' benefits, (not unemployment, housing, etc. benefits), that the IND, (Immigration and Naturalisation Service), is informed. The IND then makes a decision if the person is allowed to continue to reside in the Netherlands, and if not they have to then pay back any 'social security' payments received to date when asked to leave the country.

How on earth did I come to be in such a position? It is a very long and complex story of abusive relationships, illness and sadness because of a stillbirth and several miscarriages. Suffice to say, I had moved to the Netherlands with my second husband because of his job, together with my son from my first marriage. I was lucky to have had my son, who was premature, because I became ill during pregnancy. Two years later, quite suddenly my husband walked out. After six court cases, I had to sell my home of nine years, at a huge loss, and had to apply for 'social security'. During those nine years, I met a fantastic man whom has had faith in me and loaned me the money to complete a Masters through the Open University. Save my boyfriend and very dear friends here in the Netherlands, I am, in some respects alone now. My mother, although not the best parent in the world, died. My best friend died. My son travels for work and could be anywhere in the world for long periods of time; I do not see him often. My sister lives in Hong Kong. I have nobody to turn to and nowhere to go.

I was not eligible to vote. I watched the referendum results come in live during the night. The outcome filled me with horror; not just with regard to my future, but that of my child, my potential grandchildren and generations beyond. I am most defiantly 'in limbo'; waiting if the 'executioner's axe' will completely fall on my life in the Netherlands.

Anonymous, the Netherlands

I was born in England, and trained as a doctor in a London hospital. I came to work in Romania a year after the revolution.

Subsequently, I was asked by a priest if I could come to work in his town. In collaboration with doctors there, I worked for several years. I met my husband and we married, when Romania was not yet in the E.U. I would like to share with you what we experienced in order to marry in the UK.

At the British Embassy I had an interview with a charming gentleman who, although charged with keeping out the undesirables, realised that I and my fiancé were genuine. My fiancé was interrogated separately, but we passed the test. At the Embassy we saw many distraught couples. We will never forget the heavily-pregnant woman, weeping outside, after she was denied entry into the UK with her partner. One couple described how they were asked if they sleep together.

My fiancé received his wedding visa, and I returned to the UK to make wedding preparations. I waited at Heathrow with my family, ready to celebrate his arrival. Despite his visa, immigration officials insisted that he had not come to get married. He calmly responded, "OK, so send me back on the next available flight". They then allowed him to enter the UK. I was yet to realise that by marrying a Romanian, I had subscribed to being a member of the "undesirables".

We married. A year later we decided to settle in England but my husband was unable to obtain a spousal visa because I was unable to demonstrate my UK income and capacity to support him. I was working in Romania on sponsorship from an international drug company, and had no salary in the UK or Romania. I discussed this honestly with the Embassy, and asked if they knew of any unemployed doctors? The response was that it was my responsibility to submit the required paperwork, (even if it did not exist). If I had gone alone to demonstrate that I could earn a UK income, doubtless they would have declared that we were not a *bona fide* couple, as we were living apart.

We eventually requested a spouse visa for my husband during a UK visit on his multi-entry visa. His application "fell behind a filing cabinet". I rang Croydon, constantly. After three or more days of non-stop phoning, someone would answer the phone. They always assured us that my husband's application had been located, that it was being processed, and that within 10 days we would hear from them. We never heard more. Occasionally our hopes were raised by a phone call asking to speak to my husband and verifying that I knew his date of birth and other personal details, but the correct answers did not bring progress. Eventually a lady explained to me that promising to respond within 10 days was the procedure in that department to get rid of desperate people.

I was working long night shifts to support us both, and my health was deteriorating. Eventually, after a year, when I could cope no more, I proposed that we should approach our MP. My husband was cynical, but we did request an interview, and five days after this, his passport with the visa fell onto the mat.

After this, we had various challenges related to my Romanian stepson, who wanted to visit his dad in the school holidays. A village boy who had never before been to Bucharest, he was left crying on the street, on his second Embassy visit, because they had moved the goalposts again and wanted to reject him once more. The travelling time was eleven hours. I sent a fax to the Embassy, minutes before it closed, outlining the principles which I would expect to be applied to a kid in his position, and explaining that I would have recourse to the British press if necessary. His visa was granted, but I received a smacked wrist along the lines of, "We make the rules, and you have to swallow them". I reiterate, this is about a teenage boy wanting to visit his dad during the school holidays.

Both of us have had dual citizenship for many years, but even now we feel scarred by those experiences, and fear that these are the conditions to which we British citizens are reverting. We do not want any bona fide British-Romanian family to be subject to the discrimination, the intrusiveness, the stress and the total lack of dignity which we ourselves experienced. The future of many UK-Romanian couples is completely clouded by Brexit. We feel sad that Brexit has made the UK the laughing stock of Europe. We fear for ourselves, whether our UK pensions will have any value at all in our beloved Romania, for British society, which is breeding xenophobia at an alarming rate, and we fear for the UK economy. But, of course, the serfs will bear the brunt. "Austerity" should be re-labelled, "Oppression".

We have recently received all sorts of empty reassurances from the poor folk at the British Embassy who have been sent to muzzle us. "We will not split up families". *Really? All possible efforts were made to split US up.* "Things have changed". *No: Things DID change for a while, but now they are going back to square one, or worse.* "History shows the British always soldier on, whatever the hardships. They will get through this". *Maybe, but why on earth are we obliged to suffer this total insanity in the first place?*

E., Romania

I am devastated that my Dad voted 'leave' in the referendum, (all these migrants squeezing resources, especially the NHS… then last year he had major life-saving surgery and was looked after by said migrants, of course). What my Dad hadn't bargained for was that now Brexit has put a spanner in the works for the future of my family, too. We live in Italy. My husband and (adopted) son are Italian and we had planned to move to the UK at some point, thanks to FOM. We want to expose our son to British culture and also be close to my family, but it's not the right time yet. However, based on the UK's current hostile immigration laws, I don't think we would meet the financial requirements to live there after Brexit. That basically means that I am unable to move back to my own country, my son won't have all the experiences I had hoped for and my father will miss out on having his family around him. He is very upset about this. I talk about this and Brexit generally with my Mom in front of him. He knows I go on marches and that I am devastated at the idea of Brexit, (for myself but also for the UK and Europe as a whole), but we just can't talk about it together. Just this morning, my 4-year-old asked me whether Theresa May loves him and how come he can't go and live in England just because he is Italian and Chinese. (He wants to go and talk to the PM himself and tell her to 'behave' or he'll take her treats away!). My Dad is a party to this and it's hard to forgive.

D.B., Italy

I woke at 4am on the 24th June 2016, sobbed when I heard the news and have been angry ever since. It's exhausting and debilitating.

I grieve over the loss of an identity I have held dear since childhood. Europe and Britain have always been a part of me wherever I have lived in the world. All my childhood memories are based on life in the UK and camping holidays all over Europe. I am a British European.

All our working lives my husband and I have worked hard. We willingly paid our tax and NI contributions, proud to give something back. We worked long hours to educate our daughters, pay for healthcare – not be a burden on the state. Regardless, we were adversely affected immediately after the referendum. For what? Just to be told that our application to vote was refused despite our being within the 15 year deadline by weeks.

When our daughters left home my husband received an offer on his business and we decided to start a new venture in inland Spain. We did not want to retire and, not unnaturally, we felt confident that a move to mainland Europe, within easy reach of the UK, would provide the security and challenge we were looking for.

It took 11 difficult years to build our small hotel. By 2016, aged 65 and 73, we were winning awards and hosting guests from all over the world, (the majority from the UK), welcoming them here and bringing them together around one table, sharing our meals, their cultures and many fascinating stories.

Then the bubble burst. Our pensions lost value and we saw a significant decline in UK visitors. We now hold on to everything by a thread. Everything we have is here in Spain, our life, our home.

We see and feel the general hardening of hearts in the UK, influenced and led by a team of duplicitous, inhumane and self-serving politicians.

Appalled and ashamed by the Government's handling of Brexit, and of the Opposition's deliberate strategic inaction towards it, I mourn the Britain I knew because, undoubtedly, it is no longer Great.

I worry for our 10 grandchildren as we see their opportunities disappearing and decent values around them distorting.

Being disenfranchised fuelled my determination to keep fighting Brexit, returning to the UK to join protests and lobbying at every opportunity. I am damned if I will be silenced! When visiting the UK I connect with local people everywhere possible – of all ages and ethnic groups. I am shocked how little most know about Brexit developments. Many will be the most badly affected if we leave the EU. There is awareness work to be done.

We have only uncertainty ahead and I am eternally grateful to the EU for staying steady in the face of the UK's chaos – and to the increasing number of UK politicians who have had the courage and integrity to publicly resist Brexit.

Scarlett Farrow, Spain

★★★

I remember the morning after the referendum like it was yesterday. I sat on the sofa, clutching my 6-week-old baby, with tears pouring down my face. I was grieving.

I was grieving for the opportunities which my children, and their friends and their children, will now never have. To follow their dreams wherever they make take them. To study, travel, work and live in other cultures as easily as I have done. For the first time, I worry that my children will have less opportunities than I did and I am sorry.

I was grieving for my country, which no longer feels home. A place that, when times are tough, now looks inwards and says "me first". A place which I fear no longer welcomes me and my children, a place which no longer represents the values of tolerance and openness and empathy which I strive to instil in my family.

I was grieving for our friends in Europe, who have welcomed us with open arms, but who are not shown the same in return. Who agree the EU is not perfect but who agree a united Europe is worth fighting for.

I was grieving for the truth. Not just the lies that were told during the campaign, and not just the people who believed them without question. No, I was grieving for the truth about what it would mean to Leave. And I was grieving for the fact no-one had made a sufficiently compelling case about the benefits of staying. How arrogant we were to think the benefits were obvious. And for this lives will be shattered, the lives of real people who have made their homes and families across borders, taking for granted security and stability.

And, I admit, I was grieving for myself. Work took us to Switzerland in 2005 and, like all economic migrants, we were delighted to have the chance to pursue great jobs in what is, for us, a better place to live. We moved to France in 2012, settling here permanently in 2016. All of a sudden it wasn't sure we could stay. What would happen to our home? The kids' schools, the only life they've known so far? Our jobs? Everyone says not to worry, but it's impossible not to when no-one actually knows. It's hard not to feel betrayed by the (fortunately few) family and friends who voted "Leave".

I still hold a British passport, mainly because I have not settled any-where for long enough to be eligible for citizenship. I have benefited from the freedom of movement afforded to me as an EU citizen and have lived in 3 countries since leaving the UK 13 years ago. But I am most definitely European. I am so proud of this continent and its diversity, history, culture – and even its imperfections. I am so grateful for the opportunities it has given me and I will do everything I can to give my children, and all children, the same opportunities.

Edwina, France

★★★

I'd like to put in a word for just under half the British population, if not indeed far more than half by now, who are absolutely horrified by what is going on in Great Britain. People who love their home country, but are no longer able to identify with it. After the Brexit decision and its ratification by the British Parliament, someone said she felt as though her mother had turned round and rammed a knife into her guts. She was right – that is exactly how it feels. Especially bitter for the many hundreds of thousands of Britons living in Europe who were not entitled to vote in the referendum or the subsequent General Election because they had been abroad for more than 15 years. In many cases, our EU voting rights were the only suffrage we had – and now we are to lose these too. You can imagine, I'm sure, how heart-breaking it is to have to stand aside. To have to watch as others stride out into a wonderfully optimistic, shared – and reformed – European future, while our country slinks off treacherously, its reputation in ruins, leaving us shamefaced and bereft. Every Pulse of Europe meeting moves me to tears. The feeling of isolation is unbearable. Every time Theresa May says, 'as we leave the European Union', we feel the knife twisting. Every European flag and every European anthem reopens the wound. Britons, both at home and abroad, who are passionate EU citizens are being forced to live with this, and watch helplessly as their country plunges over the cliff. We need to thank the EU in this situation for treating us with such generosity and respect. Their efforts on behalf of UK citizens in the EU, in particular, are heart-warming and truly praiseworthy. That alone bears testimony to the greatness of the joint European project. But I would ask the citizens of Europe not to pass judgement on Great Britain and its people lightly, but to remember those who – like myself – hover permanently between grief and incandescent fury, powerless in the face of this accursed Brexit.

Anonymous, Germany

★★★

I came to Luxembourg in 1974 to work for the European Commission, a year after Britain joined the EEC. We were the pioneers, the idealists. I was 23, good at languages, but a long way from Bristol in those days. No budget airlines, the flights were expensive. No cheap telephone calls in those days, a daily call to my Mum cost the earth. No Skype, WhatsApp or Facebook. But my life changed immeasurably for the better from the day I arrived. Even though I'd refused to go to university when I was younger, I now felt I'd made the right choice: I was living abroad, surrounded by eight other nationalities all speaking their native tongues, it was fun, it was stimulating: we were working for the European "project". Native Luxembourgers were still at that time traumatized by their experiences under Nazi occupation during WWII, they would not visit Germany, a 20-minute drive away, they refused to speak German even though their local dialect, Luxembourgish (now an official language), was largely based on German. They spoke French instead.

I got married, after a few years moved to Belgium, and continued to work for the European Community in Brussels. I had children, learnt Dutch, and our colleagues now came from 15 countries. I find it difficult to describe the sheer buzz of so many nationalities interacting, sharing cultural activities, switching languages mid-sentence, getting on so well together! And it was all so normal! My children went to the European School, studied many subjects through their second and third languages and gained a vast insight into other cultures. What a wonderful opportunity.

After 13 years in Brussels and now on my own with my children, I transferred back to my beloved Luxembourg. After a few years, the EU expanded to 28 countries.

I retired after 35 years at the Commission but have loved every minute of my life as a "faceless Eurocrat". I continue to live in this beautiful country of Luxembourg, nestled between France, Germany and Belgium, each only a few minutes' drive away. Out of the world's total of 194 nations, all but 20 are represented here in a small population of half a million people. Luxembourg thrives and prospers on mass immigration, we welcome it.

My life continues to be enriched by this diversity – it has brought me much joy. My closest friends are from many different EU nations. Refugees? No problem. The suburb where we live only has 7000 people, but 94 nationalities, including 300 Syrians.

The result of the Referendum was devastating for my husband and myself. I feel totally bereft, angry, abandoned and depressed and it doesn't get any easier as time goes on. I can only describe it as having your heart ripped out of your body, against your will. Your very identity is destroyed in an instant. I have always been a proud Brit as well as a committed European but I am now ashamed of my country of birth. Like most of the British population here, I have become a Luxembourgish citizen, but my British husband is unable to undergo the rigorous language tests, (in Luxembourgish), due to serious health problems. We cannot be certain about what will happen.

I never got a vote in this Referendum. I haven't had a vote in any national election since I was 21, (I'm now 67), before I left the UK.

I, who have a lifetime of knowledge about the EU, had no say in this momentous and tragic decision.

I don't know what the future holds, or if I will continue to receive a pension, (there are no guarantees as any "agreement in principle" has to be finally agreed by all 27 Member States and the UK). Relatively few Brits still work for the Commission but my stepdaughter is one of them. She may well lose her job – it's looking more and more likely.

How often will I see my son and grandchildren when their family of five have to pay for visas each time they visit from the UK? Not to mention increased airfares.

My husband and I have campaigned and spoken to local MPs and MEPs. The overwhelming loss we feel is brutal. I have lived in the heart of Europe and have enjoyed freedom of movement for 44 years. Our children have had tremendous opportunities and their international outlook have made them employable anywhere in the world. My life has been enriched beyond all measure. I am, and always will be, European. I'm home.

C., Luxembourg

★★★

Myself aged 49, my husband Eric aged 69, and Our son Joshua aged 7, moved to Spain in June 2001; we wanted a better life for our son, and for ourselves. Eric was already retired and getting his retirement pension; we had been running a business in the UK as Eric was an inventor, and he had sold one of his products, so enabling us to buy our house in Spain.

We moved over, with our dogs and cats, and sent Joshua to our local village school; at first he struggled, but within 3 months he was chatting away in Spanish, he also found it easier to write as he is dyslexic. He struggled a bit in secondary school as a lot of people couldn't understand why, being English, he had difficulty spelling in English. He left school with no qualifications and worked for a while in the greenhouses, and in a local restaurant as kitchen and food preparation helper. He then went on an Erasmus Scheme to train as a deep sea fisherman. He moved up to Barcelona to try and find work on the fishing boats, but was unsuccessful. He then managed to find a job as a waiter, then went on to be employed in a group of restaurants and ended up running the kitchens.

We have lived a normal everyday life in Spain and have many Spanish friends, as we live in a small village on the Costa Tropical, many populated by Spanish and Moroccans with a spattering of other nationalities. When we sat and listened to the referendum results our hearts sank, we could not believe the UK had voted to leave the EU. Since then, like many other people we have lived in limbo not knowing where we stand, with healthcare, pensions, and our *residencia* if we lose our EU Citizenship. Citizens' rights still haven't been sorted out; the UK Government has used us as bargaining chips, and we still do not have certainty, despite all the assurances from the UK PM. It seems the EU is fighting for us, but the UK has abandoned us.

Our son is going to go for Spanish Citizenship, but is having to save up slowly and do it bit by bit, as my husband and I are on the basic pension, and now the exchange rate is so bad we do not have a lot of money to spare.

Both my husband and I would like to take Spanish citizenship to give us peace of mind, but my husband is now 86, with memory problems and he would not pass the exams. I would pass the exams but at present haven't the spare money to afford it.

I have managed to keep myself sane by working to try and stop Brexit and lobby for citizens' rights.

Val Chaplin, Spain

★★★

Where to start. We, (me, hubby, toddler son and my mum and dad), moved to France in 2007. We were going to live my husband's dream – his own farm, milking goats. It was not easy with the French bureaucratic red tape and paperwork, a lot of hard work, sweat and tears but we were getting there. Fast forward to 2014 and the area suffered a parasite infestation and we lost well over half our herd. We didn't have the finances to replace them and, following advice from our accountant, before they declared us bankrupt, we had to give up. A few months of real hardship before hubby got a job at a local abattoir on minimum wage. We live a simple life so this is enough to keep us going. Perhaps no longer living the dream but we are happy and love where we are and the French way of life.

2016 and the EU Referendum. Watching it all unravel from our bubble in France, it never occurred to me that so many would believe the Leave campaign and vote for the UK to leave. I tried to do an 'all-nighter' to see the result and when things started to look bad I gave up and slept. So it was not really a shock, more a surprise, when I woke and heard the actual result. Shouting at the telly, "What are these people thinking, how can they possibly think that being out of the EU could be good". It was then no surprise that Mr Cameron then resigned. The press really started their attacks then whilst the Tories chose their new leader so that it was only possible for Mrs May to be the new leader.

Then there she stood chanting "Brexit Means Brexit", and then Amber Rudd and her Register for EU Citizens just like Germany and France in the 1940s. This appeared to be the release needed for all those xenophobes to come out of the woodwork. Britain turned into a racist country being spurred on by right-wing press who even referred to Judges as traitors.

This is not the Britain I recognise, I have always thought the British to be kind, open-minded and fully tolerant of others, a leader for others to follow.

I am now branded a 'snowflake' for standing up for Citizens' Rights, not just for myself as a British in the EU27 but for all citizens across the European Union including Britain.

I am angry, upset, anxious and worried all at the same time. My son is now 13 and well integrated into French school and way of life, he wants to be a *gendarme* when he grows up for which he must have French Citizenship – no problem as an EU Citizen. By the time he reaches 18, when he can apply, if Brexit goes ahead, he will then be a 3rd Country Citizen and the process is much more difficult and expensive. So thanks to Brexit, my son's dream is as good as over as we won't have the money to help him.

Jan, France

★★★

We bought a tumbledown house in Portugal in 2008, spent the next 5 years repairing, restoring and getting it ready to live in. We were both in full-time employment in UK then, both on good wages. I was a private healthcare worker and my husband was a lorry driver.

My husband started having some issues with his hands, he couldn't grip things. The doctor thought he had carpal tunnel syndrome; anyway, turns out he has myotonic dystrophy. A degenerative muscle wasting condition, no treatment, no cure. He was medically retired from work, too young to draw a pension, got a reasonable payout from his company.

He applied to see if he could get some disability benefits from the State but was point blank refused. Although his condition is life changing and will drastically shorten his life expectancy, no, they would not pay anything. We did appeal but got nowhere.

As I was near retirement, (I'm older than him), I had already frozen a year of my state pension, so I retired and we moved to Portugal in 2015. I had a small private pension, drew 25% cash and took a yearly income about 1500 plus my state pension. We were in rented accommodation so no house to sell for capital. But with my two pensions and growing all our own veg with chickens we were fine till Brexit!

Exchange rate drop clobbering us badly, our income vastly reduced. Used our savings so that we only had to draw my pension once a year, thus hoping to avoid too much loss.

Will never go back whatever happens, couldn't spend the rest of our lives struggling in UK on benefits, at least this way with frugal living we keep our pride. I am in touch with many of my old friends and cannot believe how the country of my birth has changed.

My family have seen a lot of Europe, my daughter actually lives in Sweden. She's married with two boys. I could not believe the vote either, my in-laws, both parents and my husband's brother and his wife voted to leave. Parents in-law are incredibly racist, they voted out because of the immigrants.

Anne Randerson, Portugal

My husband and I finally retired to a Greek island in 2011, having held the dream since 1987. The fulfilment made easier by the UK being members of the EU.

It has been rather a rocky ride with the "Greek Crisis" and, at one stage, the rise in popularity of "Golden Dawn" made me feel uncomfortable, but fortunately Greeks, on the whole, have a huge sense of *philoxenia*, (a tradition of love and hospitality towards strangers) and we certainly feel "at home".

I now prefer to adopt my Greek name, have no wish to return to the UK and wish I could apply for Greek citizenship, but that appears to be almost impossible. I THINK we might qualify to stay as "third country nationals" but that is not clear and could be marginal! We have friends who own their own home here but who won't qualify under those rules and they have grandchildren here! Another friend, who is British, is in partnership with a Greek-Albanian and they rent and have children; what will happen to them? Another friend born in the UK, worked in Sweden but still has a British passport, has children in Sweden and is married to a Swede, has a Swedish pension and rents; what will happen to him? Some "Leavers" rent, own villas, run businesses, will they qualify to stay? They don't seem concerned! They might not realise but they are "In Limbo" too, but there is one "certainty" and that is "nothing is agreed until everything is agreed", as we keep being told!

Only the other evening, with recent news of the suspension of talks, the Greek music played and I couldn't stop the stream of tears running down my cheeks.

C.C., Greece

★★★

I so empathise with the feelings of rage. For my part, I think I'd add grief, too. I really do feel bereft, not just potentially of my EU citizenship – I'll find a way to keep that – but of my country. Not only in the sense that I may eventually have to renounce my British citizenship if push comes to shove, but also I feel I have lost part of my identity. I can't identify with the xenophobic nastiness and anti-democratic posturing that seems to be rampant in the UK at the moment and the loss of respect for my compatriots hurts.

Agnes Miller, Spain

I met my wife whilst on a business trip. After several dates we both expressed our wish to take our relationship further but, as the breadwinner working in the UK, it was a case of my place rather than hers, plus I wanted to see if she could really adjust to life in the UK having been a farmer's daughter in a remote part of China. We applied for a visa which meant going through some unbelievable hoops, paying thousands in legal fees and a paying supertax, over and above the many thousands I had paid every year in income tax, so that my wife would be allowed to use the NHS. After four months she obtained a fiancé visa valid for six months by which time we would either have to get married or she would need to leave the UK. We married in June 2013 in England and shortly afterwards she obtained a residence permit valid for five years as long as she remained married to me.

I am 64, a UK citizen who retired due to ill health in 2016 having worked for 42 years and paid taxes every year. My son is 3 and is a UK citizen, like me born in England. My wife is 45 and a Chinese citizen. She is a very good full-time mum and also qualified in traditional Chinese remedies.

We now live in Amsterdam, oddly completing on our house purchase there on the day of the referendum. My wife has immediate family in Amsterdam to whom she wanted to be able to turn for support should she need it, in supporting me through my illness. She does not have that same family support in the UK. My wife has been granted a Dutch resident card valid for five years and renewable under current legislation. But to obtain this status she/we had to make the huge decision that she would have to sacrifice her UK residence status as she is not allowed to claim residence in two countries. Her Dutch residence card currently allows her free movement between EU states.

My son and I are currently allowed to live in Holland by virtue of being EU citizens. If forced to leave Holland, my son and I would have to return to the UK. However, as my wife no longer has UK residence status, we would potentially be split up as a family with my young son being separated from his mother who may be allowed to remain in Holland, or who may be forced to return to her native China. If forced apart and something happened to me, what would then happen to our son? He would be in the UK without either parent. So we feel very much in limbo and unable to make decent plans since we have no idea what the politicians have in store for us. This is particularly worrying as my son starts school in September 2018 and certain schools are available to permanent residents, others are only available to those spending a few years in Holland. So which way do we go?

It's just a mess, why can't the UK government simply allow us to go on living as a normal family, a basic human right that we have now, but because we have become a bargaining chip in this mad gamble that the UK Government is playing, we may have this basic human right stripped from us.

Keith, the Netherlands

★★★

I left the UK in November 2004, to join the father of my son and be a family. Until June 2016, I owned a small business that imported from the UK, sending orders to Austria, the Netherlands, Belgium, Germany and Italy.

Listening to the arguments for and against, I heard loud and clear that leaving the EU would mean leaving the customs union. This would be disastrous for my business.

After the vote, the decision to close was straightforward. All scenarios were looked at: practical, such as perishable shipments being held at port for days, rather than hours; financial, such as increased taxes, levies, insurance, commission. The figures didn't lie. There was no way to make the business viable without enjoying free movement of goods. I was relieved that the figures were so black and white. Had they been borderline, I might have been tempted to try and continue, on the off-chance that the two years of supposed negotiation actually came up with something.

A few customers contacted me to express their concern as to what they perceived, (rightly or wrongly), as anti-European sentiment. One customer congratulated me on the referendum result. "Well done," she said. "If only we could have that vote here. We've too many Muslims." This, in her eyes, was what the referendum was about.

My parents, with four young grandchildren, are in their seventies. "It's just a fuss," says my father. "Like the millennial bug. The fear is all for nothing." My mother is practical. "We'll be able to eat more fish, when the European boats aren't in our waters." I don't bite my tongue and our relationship deteriorates further.

British friends, after appointment-making, test-taking, document-translating and fee-paying, now hold dual citizenship. They are relieved to enjoy the same rights as their native-born partners and children, moving freely around the 27 member states as their personal and professional lives dictate, availing themselves of the legal and civil rights and freedoms with which they have grown up.

But not me. I am autistic. My autism is something that few people would guess at. It's not something that I readily admit to, as I have concerns that if I do, I shall be denied citizenship. My concerns are not unwarranted; many countries, (Canada, Australia, New Zealand, to name a few), have denied citizenship on the grounds of autism. My autism also severely prohibits me from fulfilling a handful of the practical requirements of applying. I'd prefer to stay in the country where I now live; it is easier for me to be autistic in the country where I now live than it has been in the past in the UK.

The stress caused by the uncertainty of my status in this country, coupled with the closure of the business and the general twists and turns of life that most families face, has taken its toll. My husband and I recently separated. Without my business, I now have to rely on his goodwill to show that he can support me and pay for my healthcare in this country. My family's future has become even more complicated.

Anonymous, EU

★★★

I am lucky. Yes, a Brit but was employed by a European organisation for 25 years so pension in £ or €, my choice, and they provide full health cover in UK or France. So why am I pissed off? First, because my home of 25 years will no longer be an automatic right to live there. Second, my son grew up in France and became as much French as British, really European. He will not have any rights to return home. But I am also very unhappy at the politics of xenophobia and days of the Empire, that both Tories and Labour are following. The arguments for separation from Europe were a distortion of reality. Back in Breckland, (my birth place), local people voted 'out' because of the large number of Polish or Lithuanian guys around the town. They saw this as taking away locals' jobs. But lack of UK Government control and oversight of working conditions is at the root. This is not EU policy but UK Government desire to drive down labour costs. So now I don't understand my country anymore – democracy is being twisted – and this makes me feel rootless. I am now European and that is being taken from me without giving me a democratic voice to protest. I will soon be French, (I hope), but I really only wanted to stay European. That hurts inside as well.

Nigel Makins, France

I lost my father in 2007, at 77, to cancer. He had been a career Army officer, and it was stints in West Germany under the NATO umbrella that opened my eyes to the beauty of pan-European co-operation. The EEC, and then the EU, seemed an entirely logical and welcome development of NATO – nations working together for peace, rather than allying against the prospect of war. A United States of Europe had to be the next stage of such an inspired process, and I have believed in it fervently all my adult life.

For me, economic considerations have always been secondary to what the EU has achieved culturally and socially. It is little short of a miracle that 28 – well, 27, as it turns out, sadly - such utterly disparate countries have managed to put aside their most parochial instincts and interests to work together for the common good. It is nothing short of a catastrophe that we, as a nation, have turned our backs on this quantum leap in the development of human civilisation; it has utterly devastated my life and darkens my existence from the moment I awake until the moment I fall asleep. I just don't know how I am going to see out the rest of my days in Brexit Britain with any kind of equanimity; it is an utter folly and tragedy and we are vastly diminished as a people.

Peter Gallon, Norfolk, UK

★★★

I'm the British granddaughter of a German who came to the UK in 1946 and am now living in Spain, so I proudly declare myself a European, an immigrant, and an EU fan.

My family's migration story began in 2012 when we decided we'd like to experience living in a different country. Spain was our country of choice, for the culture and lifestyle, and Ayamonte our town as it bordered Portugal, and who wouldn't see the benefit and opportunities of that?

In 2013 we moved. We were free to simply go, buy a house, continue running our small business, enrol our 7-year-old son in school, and for our daughter to find a teaching job. EU freedoms and rights were a privilege we took for granted and enjoyed until June 24th 2016, when our world was turned upside down.

We were devastated by the result, and I vividly remember weeping as it was confirmed the UK had voted to Leave the EU. Our futures immediately became uncertain but we couldn't get any answers as to how exactly we'd be impacted. Could we continue to run our business from Spain? Could we even stay in the country? What about our son's education? Our pensions? Healthcare? The questions were endless. Not many of them have been answered and even less is assured whilst walking away with 'no deal' continues to be an option. Our lives remain in limbo and our ongoing stress and anxiety very real. The cruelty for us is heightened because our town is a "Eurocity", that is the EU, via the EGTC, (European Group of Territorial Cooperation), recognises the three cross- border towns of Ayamonte in Spain and Castro Marim & Vila Real in Portugal as a single entity that can work on joint initiatives and projects, and apply for funding. This means joint tourism & jobs initiatives, and may in the future even include a shared hospital. We believed our children, who are both now multilingual, would benefit from the opportunities living in this area would present, but we've learned from the Withdrawal Agreement as it stands, that their rights to move and work anywhere in the EU will end. Worse than that, their rights to live and work in the Portuguese part of our single Eurocity will end. Our rights will be taken away from us. We'll effectively be trapped not only in our host country, but in half of our cross-border town. It's simply intolerable.

My children have been betrayed by those who promised us that nothing would change, that we wouldn't lose any rights, and they had no say in it. Their futures limited for no discernible benefit. How can it be right or moral to betray children in such a way? How can the British government, whose primary responsibility is to protect them, let them down so badly?

Forgiving those who campaigned for this is close to impossible and for those who voted for it, a daily battle. Sadly for us, this includes parents & close family members. Brexit has torn our lives apart.

Karen Kendrick, Spain

★★★

IN LIMBO – a matter of mind over matter in order to survive

Grief, frustration, despair and helplessness are all emotions that I have felt on a regular basis thanks to being abandoned by a country that I used to be proud to call my own and once upon a time my home.

My husband and I have worked all over the world but returned to Europe 12 years ago to work the remainder of our advancing years and to ultimately retire here. Seemed a sensible choice with the freedom of movement between the countries which was essential particularly for my husband in his work. I was perhaps a little more flexible as a then radio journalist, PR consultant and writer. I had, however, decided to take up teaching; a way of keeping my hand in with my communication skills and a way to use my linguistic skills. Nothing, however, prepared us for the shock of the referendum or of the following months, now turning to years, that have left us unsure as to what the future will hold. With little choice but to put my head down and immerse myself in the German language and take the subsequent tests required in order to stay in the country; my husband, in his retirement, had never expected to find himself needing to learn another language at such a level. Despite a near photographic memory, he battles with the grammatical side of languages and a fear of speaking them. Having battled on, achieved the tests and been advised that I should be successful in obtaining German citizenship, it is still a time of intense worry and stress since neither of us had ever considered returning to the UK. It was never even on our radar. I am profoundly grateful for the belief and faith our German friends and colleagues have in us as individuals since they clearly think the UK has lost its way. Its inability to provide us with the reassurance that would be expected of a home country is beyond their and our comprehension. A referendum that denied us the right to vote since having been gone more than 15 years, it seems we were considered irrelevant to the decision. Yet we were among the very people that it would affect the most. Little wonder then that German citizenship has become so important to me since this is my country now.

Now, we find ourselves wondering what will happen. Empty promises by the British government that 'this or that' may be agreed to have, so far, come to nothing. Will the pensions and medical situations be forthcoming or not? Will the freedom of movement continue? When one has worked hard all one's life and budgeted carefully for retirement, we now find ourselves in what should be the supposed 'twilight' years, continuing to work to ensure that should we be totally abandoned we may find a way to ensure we continue to support ourselves. Fortunately, hard work never scared either of us. A good thing given the rampant lack of decision by the British Government to date.

Our lives have been here in Europe for the past 12 years and no amount of hearing 'we are discussing this with Brussels' does anything to alleviate our anxiety. In fact, each time we watch the news we wonder what will be the next statement that will spout forth from a politician's mouth that will put us into an even deeper state of despair than previously. Presentations from various groups in the EU that are endeavouring to provide support and guidance may mean well. Sadly, in reality, they have no better clue than we or even the Consulate representatives who put in their pound's worth at these meetings, as to what will happen. We have been left in limbo, we have been deserted, we have been left to paddle without knowing where we are paddling to or even if we will be able to paddle long enough to survive.

F., Germany

★★★

My whole life fell to pieces at that moment on 24th June 2016 when the referendum result was announced and every day brings further torment.

I love the spirit of European co-operation: the sense of difference but togetherness. I run a consultancy business, (UK registered and taxpaying), and one of the most enjoyable parts of my work, and a selling point in my skill set, is sharing knowledge and good practice across Europe. I also exercised my right as a citizen to settle in a corner of France where I am at home. "And you will be able to stay there", say Brexiters as if that was the end of it (normally accompanied by insults about wealthy expats who retire to the sun).

My husband is indeed retired but we are not wealthy. We notice the 23% drop in the value of his pension just as much the 23% drop in my earnings and the accompanying rise in the cost of running the business. I notice the lost contracts, such as a major project with a Lithuanian research Institute and working for a Dutch company who were delighted with my services and offered to pay more than I had been charging them – my last day working for them was 22nd June 2016! I used to employ one person in the UK but I don't any more, (another bit of collateral damage). If I lose the right to freedom of movement I will have no option but to close a viable business. At my age, in a rural area, other job opportunities are few.

One irony is that we have gone from being the JAMs, (just about managing), that Mme May promised to support, to people who may fall below the minimum income level and be viewed as a potential burden on the state when our application for French citizenship is examined.

If I cannot become a French citizen I no longer know who I am. Stripped of my European identity I would indeed be stateless. My heart bleeds for friends and family in the UK and I can no longer feel allegiance for a state that treats its own people in this way. I'm angry about all of this, angry about the lies and arrogance that will result in misery for so many, sad for the future that is being denied to the young people of the UK, afraid for my own future and afraid about the kind of world Brexit is creating.

Gill, France

★★★

Our story....

My husband had searched for a position through Googling one day "Theatre Manager jobs in Malta", knowing it was English speaking, thinking it might be fun to live somewhere else. We both worked long hours with little reward – Phil in a private hospital, and me in retail, and figured it was worth a shot.

We heard he had got the position late October, put our house on the market and sold our home in a week, with 7 weeks to gather up our lives ready for a new start in January 2015. We drove to Malta with our then 19-year-old cat, suffered a severe car crash en route but arrived in one piece, in the worst winter in Malta for 35 years, on 20th December 2014.

I was absolutely devastated when hearing the result of the referendum but it wasn't totally unexpected having followed the UK news and the Leave campaigners from Malta. The best thing for me personally on the day of the news was the support network around me ... not friends and family back home (friends I have now lost), but my new Maltese 'family' at work. They understood my anguish from day 1 and they were probably more surprised than me at the result. Phil has tried to be pragmatic with me and remain positive. When I try and discuss the whole sorry state of affairs and the absolute mess the UK will be in, and the fear of being forced to return somewhere I don't want to be any more (because I have to talk about it because I don't feel heard), my family back 'home' has a favourite saying of "I'm sure you'll be OK, it won't come to that….." Friends on Facebook who always followed our pictures of sunshine and sea and updates about our new life – stopped dead June 24th 2016.

I have to visit the UK for work now every couple of months and I am astounded how everyone appears to be walking around as if "nothing is happening" and sleepwalking into an abyss. I don't tend to hide my feelings, however, and try to engage with these people describing the total surprise at the lethargy and/or ignorance I witness. I was told by a friend (during a Facebook chat) of 30+ years that I shouldn't have an opinion as I left the UK behind…. I pointed out that I may have wanted to return someday ….. not if I am absolutely forced now, I can assure her (well, I would if I spoke to her again). Her reasons for leaving were racism – too many Poles where she lives and her mother jumped on that one "you've no idea Louise" ….I was brought up in inner city Leeds & Bradford where all nationalities lived in relative harmony for some considerable time. This then brings me onto the sheer disgust and disappointment I feel for the obvious increase in the permissible xenophobic and racist behaviour in my home country. I try to obtain my news coverage from the more unbiased sources from here in Malta. Disappointed at best with much of our UK national commentary. Most of all, there is lack of empathy or understanding the Brexit position this has left us both in for almost 2 years now.

So, where are we now?… Phil works long hours in a hospital and I work long hours in retail – that aspect of our lives hasn't changed much. What has changed? We came to Malta with a view to buying our own home within the first 2 years, but our sterling house sale proceeds have fallen through the roof, and continue to do so back in my UK bank account. We're both almost 4 years older, (and the cat too – a relaxed 23 year old now). I turn 50 in October and when we should be finalising plans for our future, we are completely halted and stuck in limbo. No home of our own, and too poor now to retire, and too old to return to the UK for work. Going to be working for a very long time now I suspect.... It's not fair – we didn't vote to take away our choices.

Louise, Malta

We have made Spain our home for the last 8 years and have always felt very welcome. We have a business here, our children are in the Spanish education system and are bilingual. They have both lived in Spain for longer than they lived in the UK. They have friends here, social lives, they are part of the local community. We are able to do all this thanks to the benefits of being EU citizens. We can conduct business between EU countries without cost thanks to shared agreements; groups from the UK can travel to Spain easily, without paperwork or visas and we can travel backwards and forwards between Spain and the UK for business and to visit family. Air fares are low and flights are frequent.

All this, our livelihood and lifestyle, are being put at risk by Brexit. We were devastated when the result became clear in the early hours of 24th June 2016, I thought I would never stop crying. Ever since then, for almost 2 years, we have been fighting the Remain cause in any way possible. It has taken over our lives. Our business is already suffering due to the drop in the value of the pound. and if freedom of movement stops or is restricted, and shared agreements are no longer available, it will have extremely detrimental effects and we will struggle to remain competitive. Worse still, we may be forced to leave the country we have come to love.

We will continue to fight to remain European and are determined that Brexit will not happen because we cannot envisage a life that does not involve being a part of this wonderful community that enriches life experience.

Ali H., Spain

★★★

As soon as Bruno, my French husband, was denied Permanent Residency (despite over 20 years of living there), we knew we would leave the UK. Permanent Residency is the only route to citizenship, and we felt strongly that our rights as a family would not be safe under this government without Bruno becoming British. You only have to read news articles about the number of "Skype families" in the UK to realise the brutal nature of the Home Office under the current government, and this haunted us.

The Home Office's "hostile environment" for illegal immigrants also worried us. The lines that determine whether an immigrant is legal or not are often blurred and confusing. The government surely understands that bank clerks, hospital staff, school teachers, landlords, etc. will inadvertently discriminate against non-British residents to ensure they themselves are not breaking the law. How does a landlord avoid a fine of up to £3,000 and a possible jail sentence? Do they spend time trying to determine whether a foreign national is not an illegal immigrant (this will become even more complicated after March 2019), or do they let their property to a British passport holder? If legal immigrants leave the UK as a result of the impact of this hostile environment on their lives, does this concern a government who is determined to reduce the immigration figures to "the tens of thousands", or have the new measures been designed this way?

Furthermore, we were aware that the UK has always been polarised when it comes to diversity/multi-culture and immigration, but the statistics of a sharp increase in hate crimes since the referendum were horrifying. It seems that the loosely placed lid on xenophobic and racist views, and even criminal acts, had come flying off and people who had felt sorely suppressed for many years now felt liberated to air their grievances against anyone who had an air of foreign about them. Whether this was an intended result of any/some/all of those who voted leave or not, this was the outcome, and we saw no outrage or push against it. Even from the government. In fact, the government's dialogue and actions have frequently been divisive. In the days after the EU referendum vote Dave Davis patronisingly talked of a "generous settlement" for EU citizens which led rabid keyboard warriors to assume EU nationals would be kicked out of the country with some kind of financial settlement package they should be grateful for. Amber Rudd launched a "British jobs for British people" pledge without any thought for how foreigners living in the UK would be treated as a result. Various MPs talked about our creaking health service, blaming immigration, without any acknowledgement that EU citizens and other foreign nationals working in the health service are propping it up, and totally ignoring any impact that the government's crippling austerity measures may have had.

The government's divisive and on occasion inflammatory dialogue has not stopped at foreign nationals. As a Remainer, I felt that my identity was being stripped by their words. "If you believe you are a citizen of the world, you are a citizen of nowhere. You don't understand what the very word citizenship means" said Theresa May in one of her speeches. What message does this give to those of us who see ourselves as EU citizens as well as British citizens?

We were united in our decision to leave the UK, acted swiftly and everything went smoothly. I sold my house on the first viewing, and

Bruno secured a post in Norway, (an EEA country), around the same time, which was only weeks after his rejection. Our life in the UK has gone.

Luckily, the strain Bruno and I have been under since June 2016 has brought us closer together rather than break us. I have heard of other couples who have not been so fortunate. I am immensely proud of Bruno for standing so strong and securing a great academic post and I am so proud of my little boy who has adapted exceptionally well at his *barnehage*, making friends and learning Norwegian so quickly.

The adjustment for me is harder. I wanted to return to work and build a career once my child turned 3. This will be much harder for me in a country I am still getting to know, and a language I am finding difficult. Our move is likely to have negative implications on my career development and earning capability for years to come. My feelings of loss of identity is like a bereavement. I am uprooted. I no longer belong anywhere. I'm sure Theresa May would likely blame this on my desire to be a global citizen, rather than the shocking way the government has washed its hands of those British citizens who are married to EU nationals.

I am now aiming to have French nationality through marriage in order to give me a sense of belonging, identity and to protect the unity of my family. France is more compassionate when it comes to foreign spouses. I am fortunate to have this opportunity. I have been passionate about France, the people, the culture, the language and of course the food since I was a child. It is no coincidence I fell in love with a French man. But my love for everything French is unfortunately greater than my ability to speak the language. I am currently brushing up my school French in order to pass the required test for citizenship. The worry of not passing the language test is weighing heavily and causing me sleepless nights. What if I don't pass? What if the law changes before I manage to reach the required standard? I am having the same recurring dreams I used to have when I was a student. Turning up to the exam room anxiety ridden, only to find that the exam was yesterday.

I have as much right to a family life in the UK as any other British citizen. I resent those who voted to take that away from me in the blink of an eye. I am heartbroken that the UK has been hijacked by far-right populism and the tiny majority of voters who voted to leave the EU either in spite of the xenophobic propaganda fed by the Leave campaign, or because of it. I feel resentful that Scotland voted to remain in the EU but must leave. I am Scottish, yet I will not easily be able to move to Scotland in the future with my French husband because other parts of the UK voted to leave. I lived in England for most my adult life, but suddenly I don't belong anymore.

And we are still in Limbo. We will face uncertainty at least until the negotiations are over or if I am lucky enough to obtain French nationality. I fear the bombastic, uncouth negotiating skills of the UK government may set back negotiations on citizens' rights or may leave the UK to crash out without a deal. This would leave my family in a very precarious position. It is not impossible that in the future there may not be one country in the world where my family can live visa-free. But we feel safer in the hands of the EU than the hands of the UK government.

Emma Pollet, Norway

★★★

My partner and I moved to the Dordogne in October 2014, planning to rent for six months to try it out. Before three months were up we had decided this was where we wanted to spend the rest of our lives. By April 2015 we had found and bought what we hoped would be our forever house in a small French village and were building a wonderful life here. Just over a year later along came the referendum and threw our plans and our lives into question. I am self-employed and work via the internet for UK companies. I have no idea how Brexit will impact this beyond the huge pay cut I have already taken because of the devaluation in the pound. How will VAT work? Will I still have the right even to work here in France? Will the companies I work for be happy to contract with someone in France once they're outside the EU? We haven't yet done five years here so currently can't apply for French nationality and even if I could I'm not sure I want to. I want to be EUROPEAN, not French, and after Brexit I am not even sure I want to be British anymore. I feel ashamed of Britain and the people who voted for Brexit, some of my family members among them. Brexit is destroying future opportunities for the young people of Britain who didn't vote for it and don't want it. I feel sad for my nieces and nephews who won't experience the same freedom of movement we have enjoyed until now. I feel like my life is in limbo. We try to stay positive and keep making plans and keep moving on with our lives and hope for the best but there's so much uncertainty and so much at stake.

Michelle Airey, France

★★★

On the morning of June 24th 2016 everything changed. After 12 happy years of retirement here in our small inland village, building up a full and active life and involvement with both Spanish and British communities, we were suddenly thrown into limbo. Immediate feelings were of fear, uncertainty, anger, betrayal. Then came the practical concerns of continued health care, pensions, should we apply for Spanish citizenship? What would be our future?

Almost two years later all of these emotions are still high and questions still unanswered, since we have seen no sign of reassurance that our life will be the same after Brexit, despite our being fully "legal" here, in terms of having permanent residency at the moment and being tax payers here, and my tension headaches are certainly not going away. We are pawns, victims in some senseless political game. When will someone say something to us one way or the other? When will we be able to carry on with our normal lifestyle without this nagging undercurrent of uncertainty?

The poor exchange rate has affected our pensions quite drastically, while the cost of living is slowly rising here. We are concerned for our health care in the future since we are still not sure of the continuing reciprocal arrangement between the UK and Spain. Although we are in good health now, we will need greater care as we get older and we do not wish, nor could we afford, to return to the UK.

But it goes deeper than that, in that for us it has affected relationships with friends. We have been surprised, not only at the number of leave voters of our generation in general, but also by our (fortunately few) friends here in Spain, who have emerged as leave voters. We feel disappointed and betrayed by their arrogance and complacency, and in one case even the recent acquisition of an Irish passport. There is frustration at the lack of interest or concern, as if all will turn out right for us if we just ignore it all, and the apparent acceptance even among many Remainers that Brexit is an inevitability. Also, long-standing friends from schooldays have come out of the woodwork as Brexiters on Facebook. Friendships have now been broken. Will our hard-earned retirement lifestyle ever be the same again?

Kate & Steve, Spain

★★★

Twice today I was struck by the full emotional impact of Brexit.

The first trigger was a radio extract from the opening ceremony of the 2012 Olympic Games, with a special mention for the contribution of our wonderful NHS staff. The sheer irony of what is happening to many of our EU doctors, carers and support staff, just six years later, was impossible to bear, and once again I found myself in tears!

The second trigger was a speech given during the naturalisation ceremony for an EU citizen living in England. Listening to Britain being described as a proud and democratic country with the particular benefits of tolerance, fairness and freedom – in my opinion, the exact opposite of the direction the UK is taking at present – vividly highlighted the new ambivalence in my feelings towards the land of my birth, and instead of producing the old glow of pride, now only made me feel nauseous and angry. This time it was hearing the National Anthem that caused the tears. My beloved Jerusalem and Land of Hope and Glory have always had that effect, but now I cry from a deep sense of loss rather than for sentimental reasons.

I was born in Rutland and grew up in the UK. During my year abroad from university, I met my German husband. As his work made living in the UK impossible, Hamburg has been my home since we married, 45 years ago.

People in Hamburg traditionally have a soft spot for anything British, so it has always felt a bit special, being British here, but I have never felt the glow of belonging to the United Kingdom so strongly as in the days following the 2012 Games.

The feeling of shock and sadness among Germans at the abrupt ending to what they had thought of as a long-standing mutual love affair is, therefore, hardly surprising. People here were almost as shocked as I was when I went to bed on the night of the referendum, secure in the poll-inspired conviction that we would remain in the EU, only to wake and hear that we were OUT. I vividly remember the feeling of vertigo as the ground fell away. My heart lurched and my mouth went dry, as everything I believed in was placed neatly beyond my reach. We would no longer be part of an exciting European future. We would no longer see the Union Jack flying proudly alongside its 27 European counterparts. We would be doomed to watch as Europe moved on without us. I have never felt so abandoned or betrayed – particularly since I and many thousands of others were excluded from the referendum by the 15-year rule, thereby having our EU rights removed and our identities demolished without even having a say in the matter.

Far from revelling in my Britishness and identifying with our former national characteristics, I now find that I relate more strongly to today's German values, not least of inclusiveness and unassuming 'pride in not being proud'. I am now no longer happy to tell people where I come from. I am ashamed of the enmity being shown towards EU citizens in the UK, ashamed of the tone used by many Leavers in the social media, ashamed of the Government's attitude and behaviour towards the European Union, and particularly ashamed of the extraordinary accusations made in certain newspapers, as if we were once again at war, rather than being fair negotiating partners on equal ground.

Bereft of all the things I loved about my British identity, and desperate to retain my EU rights, I have now taken German citizenship, something I would never have done without Brexit. I always felt that although I loved Germany, nationality was a matter of the heart, and that my British passport was essential to my personality. Brexit has put paid to that.

I am thankful that this path was open to me, unlike many other UK citizens in Europe and EU citizens in Great Britain. I dare not even imagine how it must feel for those who do not have this opportunity, knowing what the emotional impact has been for me.

Through my new German status, I am once again safe in the arms of the EU, but my heart is broken, and I feel I have forfeited my identity. I am constantly amazed by the depth and persistence of my sorrow, and find I am permanently on the verge of tears. Never in my life have I felt so vulnerable.

Rosemary, Germany

★★★

On the night of the Referendum, I was on a panel on Deutsche Welle TV with other British people in Berlin, commenting on the results through the night. I had a strong suspicion that the result would go the wrong way and it was clear early on that Leave had won. We left the studio the next day, numb, at 7am. I couldn't get the idea out of my head that I would have to stand in a different queue to my family at the airport. It was symbolic of my new status – they would all be EU citizens but I wouldn't. That evening I went to the country with two of my best friends and our children; one of them told me that she had woken up that morning to the news and cried for me, knowing how it would affect me. There was a huge storm that evening: it seemed fitting as the sky turned black and the wind howled, like Armageddon. By 10pm I just had to curl up and go to bed, I simply couldn't talk anymore.

So it was like a bereavement. On a personal level, I had to ask myself how I related to my country. I verged from wondering if I belonged anymore to wanting a divorce. I'm actually more patriotic than I thought – we went back to the UK for the 2012 Olympics, I watched Andy Murray win his first Wimbledon on dodgy Wi-Fi in Greece, and we have a problem in our house when Germany plays England at football! Plus, I've always been proud of the things the UK does well – music, comedy, literature, TV – and I thought that we actually hadn't done a bad job as a multi-cultural society. Apparently, the latter appears to have been wishful thinking, as, post-Referendum, some nasty attitudes were unleashed.

I reflected a lot on what it meant to be European and British. I have always felt European since I was young: it was the way I was brought up but also my personal feeling. I believe that our diversity in Europe, mixed with our shared history and culture, can make us stronger. So I wanted to see what it was like to live and work in other European countries and at 14 I decided I was going to study law at the Sorbonne in Paris, although no-one in my family had ever studied abroad (or law).

Being European is also about intergenerational responsibility for me – to my father, who fought in WWII and father-in-law, who survived the bombing of Dresden. And my husband is from East Germany and the peaceful transition that followed the fall of the Berlin Wall owes a lot to the European project. So, for our family, Europe means peace in our time and it is these principles of peace and solidarity that we want to pass on to our children.

But I couldn't sit still and be depressed, I needed to do something. And that was why I started, with others, a campaign for British in Europe, the people who were forgotten in all this, and mostly had no say in the referendum, to give us a voice.

Jane, Germany

★★★

A few weeks ago I had a particularly Bad Brexit Day. Every day that Brexit hangs over me, is a bad day, but this was particularly miserable:

article after article about just how devastating Brexit will be for our country, citizens' rights, people's lives. What tipped me over the edge, however, were comments that Brits abroad long term should not have a vote for life since they are no longer invested in their country.

I burst into tears and cried out my whole frustration with my disenfranchisement, my sense of invisibility, and at the ugly shadow cast over my life as Briton living in the EU with a non-British family. I am devastated that I may not be able to move back to the UK with my Italian family in the future.

The UK's unfair immigration laws are so family-UNfriendly and may well prove too stringent for us to meet after Brexit, and I will not be able to be close to my ageing parents and other family members. I will not be able to immerse my son in British culture. I will be effectively exiled from the country of my birth.

It's probably not a good idea to get hold of your bank card while in a highly emotional state, but I did. I bought myself a plane ticket I can't really afford for the Great Northern March to protest against Brexit, which took place in Leeds at the weekend.

I'm a British citizen with no parliamentary representation yet my life is being turned upside down. That's why I travelled to yet another protest on Saturday. I have to shout my outrage on the streets to try to get someone to hear me.

I completed my Master in Translation 20 years ago in the very city of Leeds. My first steps as I emerged from university took me to the Secretariat of the European Parliament in Luxembourg, where I completed a three-month traineeship as a translator, supported by an allowance. What an incredible experience. What a fantastic opportunity, serving as a springboard for my career and broadening my cultural horizons.

I am still friends today with people I met there from all over the EU. What a profound loss that such educational and cultural opportunities will no longer be available to young people.

During those three months I saw from an insider's perspective the breadth of topics addressed by the EU, I learned about the decision-making process, read minutes of committee meetings and reports and sat in on a plenary session of the European Parliament. I saw BRITISH MEPs. How I wish folk in the UK could grasp that the UK is part of a democratic process and does not have decisions foisted on it by 'foreign bureaucrats in Brussels'. We are part of a family of nations. We are always part of the entire process and the whole mantra of 'taking back control' is completely baseless. Instead, so many, like myself, are LOSING control of their lives, thanks to Brexit.

D.B., Italy

★★★

For more than 50 years I dreamed of retiring to France, ever since as a single teenager I went to play rugby in the foothills of the Pyrenees in the south west. I was enchanted with the beautiful countryside and the friendliness and hospitality of the people. I was too poor to even consider buying a place in those days but the dream never left me.

Move on 25 years and my wife and I holidayed in Brittany. It was her first visit to the country and, like me, she fell in love with it. Several holidays later – this time in the Charente – we determined to make what was my dream, but now our dream, come true. For two years we rarely went out as every spare minute was spent working and saving for our dream. We started a property search online and followed that with visiting places while on holiday. And then we found our cottage in a tiny six-house hamlet and within two months, it was ours, paid for out of the overtime I did.

We used it as a holiday home, visiting two or three times a year. It was our plan to move there full-time when we retired. Meanwhile we worked on improvements, cutting the jungle of a garden, painting walls, laying floors, creating bedrooms... Bit by bit, as money became available, the place got more comfortable, more homely and more to our liking.

And then we were hit by a double whammy: my brother-in-law, suffering from multiple sclerosis, deteriorated until now he needs constant 24-hour care and my wife is his main carer; and the second hit was Brexit. On their own, they wouldn't be such major obstacles. We could delay our permanent move to France but Brexit means delay is no longer possible. With the uncertainty of our rights once we leave the EU, who knows when, or if, we'll be able to move into our retirement home? Without Brexit, we could continue visiting regularly but, as seems likely now, there'll be no free movement and so travelling may require visas and restricted lengths of stay. Our dream has become a nightmare.

Ian Williams, Charente, France

★★★

24th June 2016. The unthinkable was happening. A quick glance at my phone in the middle of the night confirmed my worst fears; we were going out. For six months before I could only watch from the sidelines and hope for the best. Having been in the Netherlands for over fifteen years I had been denied the right to vote, and now I had to face the full consequences of the result on my own. I stayed up all night and by the time my kids had woken up I was weak and emotional. Why was daddy crying? How could I explain to my children that the EU was the very foundation of our life; that they wouldn't even exist if it wasn't for the EU?

My father was born during a bombing raid in 1940. A few years later he was saved from drowning by a German prisoner-of-war who was working on the family farm. And now, a generation later, here I am, living happily in a peaceful Europe with my German girlfriend and our three half-German, half-British kids. What a privilege and honour it is to enjoy this hard-earned peace. How lucky we are.

It was the EU that gave my girlfriend and I the opportunity to each follow job opportunities to the Netherlands. It was the EU that brought us here, and brought us together. It is the EU that allows us to raise our children here. I've often wondered how my half-German, half-British kids, living in the Netherlands, will identify themselves in the future. After the Brexit vote I wonder if they will be as proud to be British as European? Until now the two went hand in hand. And how will they view Theresa May's 'citizens of the world are citizens of nowhere' remark? I like to think that they will prove her 100% wrong.

And yet, right now, as a Brit in Europe I do feel like a citizen of nowhere. My own government doesn't care about the likes of me. We have been disenfranchised, abandoned, abused even. It's one year after triggering Article 50 and our Citizens' Rights, the rights that allow us to live and work where we do, are still on the negotiating table. I often feel a sense of rage and disgust towards the whole situation: the folly of the ill-conceived referendum, the lies, the division, the partisan press and the revival of ugly nationalism. I wrestle daily with the knowledge that half of my family in England voted Leave. I know they didn't vote to hurt me, but still the pain is almost physical. Incredibly they didn't even know that their vote could put my family and me in such an uncertain and worrying position. And if they, my own family, didn't know the full consequences of their vote, what does that tell us about the rest of the voters across the country?

We all live under the same sky. No matter what happens, in the end I know I am not a citizen of nowhere; I am a citizen of the world.

Anonymous, the Netherlands

PART III

*"I have been worried each and every single
day since the Referendum"*

I have seen comments about pensioners in the sun getting their comeuppance with Brexit, obviously by people jealous of those brave enough to attempt to make a new and better life for themselves. Those commenting also seem to assume that that we all live in grand villas and spend our lives lazing around our pools. There are some people who have that life, and I am sure most of them worked really hard and deserve their comfortable retirements, but a lot of us came to Spain not because we were rich but actually because we were, (relatively, by European standards), poor.

I spent a lot of my life on a minimum wage, I've done cleaning, bar work, shop work. I worked hard, double shifts sometimes, feet killing me, and yet I always worried about the electricity bill, was always struggling/juggling with money. When I looked for some help, because I had a child at home at the time, I was told by someone in social services to stop all work as I would be better off on benefits. I refused and carried on working as I was then, and wish to remain, independent. I did evening classes and got a book-keeping qualification, I was above minimum wage, but not that far above. I had a mortgage and although my head was above water now I could never earn enough to save significantly for my old age.

My daughter left home, years passed, retirement loomed, and contrary to looking forward to it – although I would welcome not working as I was getting older – I could see no way it was a possibility for me.

On a basic UK pension I would go back to worrying about the electricity bill, I would be one of those pensioners who had to choose between heating and eating. I would have no money for pleasurable things, no quality of life. I started looking into the possibility of living in a different country, where my pension would go further and I could still enjoy life. In my middle sixties I decided to leave everything I knew and start learning a new language.

I sold a one-bedroomed flat and bought a small two-up two-down terraced house in Spain, no access to a pool, all very basic. I was careful to leave myself with a little 'cushion' so that I could visit my daughter and friends once a year. I wouldn't be able to afford any other holiday, but I was living near a beach anyway, and I could afford a monthly coach trip out. I was retired at last, yet I didn't worry about bills, and I could afford to socialise. I was happy and relaxed, I thought all those years of struggle were behind me. That lasted a whole year and one month.

Then came Brexit and the plunge in the pound. I'm not stupid, I did realise exchange rates fluctuate, but I didn't expect the rate to sink, and pretty much stay sunk. My quality of life is now like the one I had imagined as a pensioner in the UK and sought to escape. Basically I can still live, although I worry how low the rate will go come March 2019, but I can't have all the extras that make life enjoyable. I socialise still, but I play cards with friends, or go on walks, rather than meals out. I still do some things, but everything has to be weighed and measured against the incoming bills, and adjusted accordingly. And don't think it doesn't get cold in Spain in winter, or so hot in the summer it's hard not having the air-con on because once again the electricity bill is a worry in my life.

The cushion is slowly being eroded, I am frightened for the future, and I am not the only one living like this. We are in limbo, after over six hundred days we still don't know if we will have reciprocal health care, or whether our pensions will be frozen. Nothing's decided until everything's decided. It's there on the table, but it's not definite, so I won't go to see my daughter or old friends now in case I need that money to pay for an operation. I am getting old, I am not going to get any healthier than I am now. I have no idea what I would do if I needed long-term treatment and it wasn't available. I simply wouldn't be able to afford it. I would not have put myself in this position, I was trying to better my life not make it worse. I can't go back as I can't even buy back my one-bedroomed flat, and I wouldn't get any help as I would have been deemed to have made myself homeless. I am depressed and so worried about the future, for me personally, but also for Britain, which seems to be taking a nasty insular path.

All financial concerns aside, being part of Europe meant a lot to me. I grew up on my parents' war stories, and peace and trade in a united Europe was always the future to me and why I voted IN in 1975 and REMAIN in 2016. I still can't believe Britain is turning its back on that, it's like a bad dream from which I can't wake up.

B.T., Spain

★★★

My name is Adam, I am twelve years old and live in France with my Mum, Dad and Nana. I have half-sisters and brother who live in England – they are much older than me.

I go to college and will be starting in *5eme* in September. I started school when we moved to France and I was just two and three-quarters. I learnt French very quickly. My best friend, Romain, is French. In fact nearly all my friends are French.

We live on a farm and have pigs, ducks, chickens, a sheep and a cat and two dogs (they are my pets).

At the moment, when I grow up I want to be a *gendarme*. I am not sure they will let me after Brexit, but this is all I have ever wanted to do. I know I could go back to the UK when I am old enough to be a Policeman, but that would mean leaving my Mum and Dad. And I do not think the UK will understand my exam certificates. What if I want to do something that would mean me going to another country in the EU for education or to work? I also want to get the best exams and education I can here in France. After Brexit will France still let me go to school here?

I worry about what is going to happen to my Mum and Dad, they do not speak French as good as me and I know they would never pass an exam in French so could never get French Nationality. What is going to happen when my brother and sisters want to visit me for Christmas, also my Aunty comes every holiday and spends time with my Nana who is now getting quite old – she could never manage having to move back to the UK if we had to go back, it would kill her.

Adam, France (now aged 13)

★★★

I'm sure I'm not alone when I say Friday morning 24th June 2016 was one of the worst moments of my life. I remember the silence of the early morning and the whirr of my computer, the feeling that my heart had jumped out of my body with shock then the black despair.

My European adventure began many years earlier when I went to Norway in 1995 to work as a district musician for 8 years. Although Norway is not part of the EU, they interpreted their very close referendum result by trying to unite around a compromise rather than split the country even more, as the UK government has done, and became part of the EEA. As a result, I was able to use freedom of movement and to live and work there as an EU citizen. I now realize that, had I not been an EU citizen, I would maybe only have been able to stay there for one year because as a non-EEA citizen I would not have been able to accept my second post, as there were EEA citizens applying for it who would have had priority. In fact my Hungarian colleague, (not EU at the time), an amazing flautist, got a job in Norway but had to wait 2 months while they made sure there were no EEA citizens suitable for the post. It makes me numb with rage that this will be the fate of future British citizens if Brexit goes ahead. So many closed doors and clipped wings.

After Norway I spent almost 3 years in Poland teaching English, and was there when they entered the EU so I only needed one initial visa. It was tedious getting it and involved going to the Polish Embassy in London, queuing for several hours in the rain, and paying quite a lot of money. I went back to Poland last year and the border control was gone with only an EU sign, saying Poland, in its place, just as simple as going from county to county. It brought tears to my eyes and it felt like the very symbol of freedom. Schengen is a wonderful thing!

Anyway fast forward to June 2016. I am in Italy and have been here for 10 years. My first real shock was discovering that as I had only been domiciled and not resident, I had not been exercising treaty rights and so those 10 years counted for nothing as far as my status was concerned. I immediately got residence on the Monday after the referendum and also changed my driving license to an Italian one. I have been constantly worried about the cut-off date and the UK's continual threat to "just walk away" or "no deal is better than a bad deal". All I can do is wait and hope that I will be able to continue my path to permanent residence and citizenship. It feels like my last chance of freedom, of getting an EU passport and being able to keep my European citizenship. Although I have always been made to feel very welcome and my Italian friends are genuinely baffled as to why I should be worried, I do worry a lot and feel under constant pressure to prove myself and be a valuable immigrant. For the first time, I feel foreign and the anger that my own country have thoughtlessly caused so much suffering to so many people, EU citizens in the UK and British in Europe, is sometimes overwhelming.

Perhaps, the worst part of this nightmare is the fact that my own parents voted leave as well as some other members of my family. They did so in good faith and after years of reading the Daily Telegraph, but my mother refuses to acknowledge any of my problems due to Brexit and continues even now to say things like "well now we can control our own laws and won't be dictated to by Brussels". It has caused huge tension between us and I feel I have lost my mother in a way. That is the hardest part of this for me.

Ellie, Italy

★★★

Where to begin I wonder?

The last few months have seen increasing reports of horrible racism and xenophobia in the UK and I am saddened to my core by them. My generation supported "Rock against Racism", we fought against the National Front. I had hopes those days would never return.

I left the UK for a new life in Greece, nearly a quarter of a century ago. It was the light at the end of a long dark tunnel for me. I am unable to work because of ill health and I live on a very small income. It will be many more years before I qualify for a retirement pension.

I'm fortunate enough to be able to live amongst people who have welcomed me into their society, homes and families. My neighbours and friends have been kinder to me than I deserve; not laughing at me when I struggled with the strangeness of the language. Kind people who offer friendship and hospitality to strangers, the concept of Greek Philoxenia.

Not once in all these years has anyone said anything remotely xenophobic to me, or made me feel unwelcome. This makes it all the more shocking to me the way that friends from the 3 Million EU27 are being treated in the UK.

Along with many other people I have been very worried each and every day since the referendum, losing sleep. Each discovery makes my situation seem worse. Lots of people have the option to apply for citizenship in their adopted home, sadly Greek citizenship isn't available to people without Greek parentage. Property ownership is also going to be a problem when the UK withdraws. It will become an expensive legal nightmare.

I am frustrated to the point of tears trying to get my family and friends to understand my position, the reactions have been on a scale from the obvious platitude of "You have a British passport so you will be OK!" I have asked how this is true but nothing reassuring or remotely helpful has been proffered. One now ex-friend told me that I'd "had a good run for my money and it was my turn to suffer along with them.." Unbelievable.

No comprehension or empathy from many of the other British in Greece who seem to be sleepwalking into Brexit.

L.S., Greece

★★★

June 23rd, 2016 was a milestone in my life.

Voting was over and David Dimbleby gave an initial forecast that Remain would probably win by a narrow margin. By the early hours of the morning the same presenter's face was ashen as he hoarsely announced that a narrow victory had in fact been the trophy of Leave. A two per cent margin is, it seems, enough to tear up decades of cooperation.

And then it hit me. My own people had voted away my future without even inviting me to the execution ceremony. Because I have been living for over fifteen years outside the country where I was born and raised, Her Majesty's Government decrees that I have no say in a decision which has severe consequences for me and many others. The carpet was about to be pulled from underneath us.

Brexit means Brexit. Take back control. But just what does Brexit mean?

For me, it means my Spanish permanent residence permit will become null and void once Britain leaves the EU. I could lose the right to work here, to own my flat, even to receive state healthcare. Other British citizens living here without their papers fully in order could suffer much worse. At the very least I shall have to go through a long process to reapply for the right to continue living in the country that has been my home for twenty-three years. EU citizens living in the UK face even more uncertainty.

Old school friends of mine became hostile on Facebook when I expressed my worries. A simple comment would turn into a major row, threads running into several pages. Many friends and colleagues reported that they could no longer speak to their families on the phone without a shouting match about Brexit.

My Spanish clients still give me looks of incredulity. My upstairs neighbour is aghast at Britain's decision to leave the EU and the racism that friends of hers living in the UK have been subjected to. We're not all like that, I tell her.

Time passes, and it becomes clear that Theresa May has no real plan, no real idea what she is doing, and Brexit has descended into chaos. I laugh but feel like crying. Experts are now enemies in the age of post-truth, their words ignored, scoffed at. The pound tumbles as the ever-increasing complexity of Brexit becomes clear. And yet not one politician from any major party has the courage to say in public what so many of us have known from the very beginning: Brexit is a terrible idea, and should be stopped.

Like many others, I have no idea where I stand. The British government is clearly indifferent to the well-being of its citizens living in the EU.

I feel backed into a corner, and make a tough decision. But it's the only decision that makes sense in all this madness: to apply for Spanish citizenship and in doing so renounce my British passport.
Or, as I like to call it, *My Own Personal Brexit.*

Something insane happened in the UK on June 23rd, 2016. I want nothing to do with it. Britain, if you can do a Brexit, I can too. I only hope that enough people come to their senses soon and turn things around before everything that made Britain into a wonderful place is flushed down the toilet forever.

John Bentley, Spain

★★★

I am self-employed and work in the wine business managing export sales for high-quality German wineries. My European story began 24 years ago when I went on an Erasmus exchange to the University of Giessen, Germany for a semester of study. Following this, I was offered a job in Düsseldorf with a company who worked in the import-export sector. They offered me a permanent contract post-university and I happily returned. At the time I had to apply for a residency and employment card – this was no problem as I had a job.

Over years, I have put down roots in Germany. I enjoy the openness, the lifestyle, the standard of living, the fabulous wine and the friendly people.

A couple of years ago, I had reached the point in my career where it was a viable option to be sustainably self-employed. I am very lucky to be happily making a living doing what I love. As it is still in its infancy, the business has not received full tax returns for the past three years. This means that I cannot fully prove my self-sufficiency at this moment in time. This is an essential hurdle to clear when applying for residency.

I feel like I am in limbo because there is no guarantee that Brits in Europe will be able to move around Europe (and internationally) without red-tape and costs in terms of visas. I travel extensively throughout Europe visiting customers, importers and presenting different wines. Often this travel is arranged at very short notice. Additional paperwork to enable me to travel will put a very severe strain on my business. I worry that my services will be so constrained by being unable to travel quickly, flexibly and without visas, that the viability of my business will be destroyed. If the business fails and I am unemployed there is a risk of deportation – to a country I last lived in twenty-four years ago. The agreement between the EU and the UK may protect some rights – such as being able to set up and run a business as a foreign national; however, there is lack of clarity on other points including Brits currently living in the EU being land-locked and unable to move to new EU countries should the opportunity arise. We were told that nothing would change.

In the future, my retired mother who lives in the UK alone, would love to join me and my brother (he moved to Germany four years ago). Under the new agreement, she would have to be financially or physically dependent on our support. It seems crazy that we may have to wait for her to degenerate instead of her moving as a fit and healthy pensioner.

Everyone seems to think that it will be OK – someone will work out the detail. But our MPs and MEPs are not listening. My letters receive zero-to-little response. We are people. This is not just about trade, we are negotiating the foundations of our lives and our livelihoods.

Nicola Blanchard, Germany

★★★

After a career in engineering and IT, I moved into the corporate world as a head of department. I finished the last 12 years of my working life in demanding roles in the city of London. It took a divorce late in life to finally enable me to retire.

I was in no financial position to afford to retire in the UK, so committed to refurbishing a small two-up two-down cottage in rural France where I had previously enjoyed numerous holidays. Life became worth living again with the arrival of my second wife. A new lifestyle was about to start, labelled as 'living the dream' by so many back home who were blissfully unaware of my initial problems of finding and emptying a septic tank, and how to stop the rain coming through the roof.

The night of the referendum was both a shock and a turning point. Never before had I been involved in politics or been an activist in any way. It was immediately clear to me that the British public had been misled into believing scandalous Brexit promises, but what to do? Where to turn to for reliable information? My mind was going through disbelief, anger, frustration, depression. All the planning and preparation both financially and geographically were suddenly at risk. Decisions that I had made were now irreversible, yet the rug had been pulled from under my feet.

After learning that a close relative had voted leave, I told him of the severe consequences this would create for me. His response was "Oh, I didn't realise!"

My situation has become so much more complicated with the disastrous Brexit vote, as my new wife is younger than me and has several more years to work in the UK before hopefully joining me in retirement. As this is likely to be after Brexit, the conditions she will face when moving to the EU from the UK are still totally unknown and very worrying. We could end up in a situation where I could not afford to return to the UK and my wife could find it impossible to move to France. The thought of finding it impossible to live in the same country as my wife in my final years, through no fault of our own is quite unthinkable, and has focussed my mind on fighting the stupidity of Brexit.

I find that I suffer from mixed emotions, none of them very positive, when I look at the charade that is being played out in Parliament in the name of democracy. Firstly, with the feeling of disbelief and shame at the way EU citizens have been treated so shabbily in the UK by the government and the tabloid press. Then with anger at the loss of treaty rights of UK citizens simply trying to earn a living in the EU. Being deprived of onward freedom of movement, they will lose their livelihoods, as Britons in Europe will be "landlocked" on 29 March 2019.

A recent habit of mine, which I must stop, is posting at 3am when I'm unable to sleep! The thought of the impending disaster of Brexit and the knowledge that we have a limited time to do something about it, means that it is all too often on my mind. On 31 March 2019 I do not want to find myself saying, "I wish I had done more to stop this crazy nonsense".

Brian, France

★★★

I remember the morning of the referendum result well. It is still etched or rather scarred into my mind. It was a warm morning. I had for once slept well. I was undergoing chemotherapy and feeling none too happy. It leaves you feeling, to put it mildly, distinctly uncomfortable. I was also still overcoming the after effects of two operations.

But I have jumped ahead in the narrative. To begin at the beginning. My wife Susana is Spanish and we have two children. I have two children from my first marriage; my first wife who was Belgian died young of cancer leaving me with two very young children. One day Susana walked into our lives and stayed. After some years in England, an opportunity arose to move and work in Spain, in the city where Susana was brought up. The two elder children were established in the UK and decided to stay. It is, after all, only an hour or so flight back to UK so really no problem to shuttle back and forth. The two younger children who had dual nationality could become truly bilingual, which we thought would help their prospects.

In 2002 we packed our belongings, furniture and family memories into the back of a lorry. We moved and unpacked familiar things into our new unfamiliar house one very hot May Day and thus began our new life. Curiously Spain and UK felt connected, one country, just different languages. We travelled back and forth either by plane or driving through France, apart from two kilometres it is motorway all the way. No customs checks; money could be moved back and forth and business arranged through the internet. We made friends here. I learnt to speak Spanish. The elder children now with their own children visited frequently. Life was good, very good. Then in late 2015, I was diagnosed with cancer, but curable they said. In January 2016, I underwent an operation which, whilst removing the cancer, did not turn out well and I needed a further emergency lifesaving operation. I have to say the medical team here in Spain were and are second to none. Extremely kind and efficient. As a precaution, they recommended chemotherapy for six months and regular check-ups every three months. It seemed more often as the surgeon who operated on me checked on his handiwork and the oncologists check on their work. I am not lacking in care.

So, it was that I went downstairs that June morning to check the result of the referendum on the internet, as we do not receive British TV. I read the news, I read again. I listened to BBC Radio 4. 'Jesus', I thought. 'This cannot be'. Susana came down. We sat on the sofa in disbelief. It felt as though one had been told of a death of a friend and had suffered a bereavement. I felt an acute sense of deep loss, sadness and rejection of something I thought good. Those feelings have never left me. They are still as fresh today as they were in June 2016. Thoughts rushed through my mind, can I stay, what is going to happen with my treatment? I want to stay for my treatment. If I am forced back will I get treatment in the UK? What are the rules for returning citizens? What about our home, where will we live? We could not possibly afford a similar house in the UK. Get a grip, I said to myself. Calm down, my chemo brain, as I call it, was refusing to be rational. You have two years at least before things change. There is time. At which point our daughter in England phoned. She was adamant that Brexit was not going to happen. I hoped she was right but at that stage it was of little comfort.

On the positive side, I was told, by those in the know here in Spain, that I need not worry about treatment as I would be covered come what may. The law of the province where I live ensures this. However, the residential situation was still unresolved and no lawyers could give me a definitive answer, nor could or can they still answer another niggle that I had that concerned movement of capital and receipt of my private UK pension. When the UK leaves the EU, all four freedoms will disappear and what then? We had, at least, taken the precaution of transferring capital out of UK before the pound really plunged, but there was a sufficient sum still locked up in the UK, on which we would receive a huge hit when we came to transfer it. But then I thought to myself should I transfer any money? What if I am kicked out of the country? More panic. I thought that perhaps I should become Spanish and lose my British nationality which was something that I did not want to do, just in case I had to return to UK. As if Brexit was not bad enough, Michael Howard the former Tory leader, had helpfully been suggesting the UK invade Spain to protect Gibraltar and the UK press was getting quite heated about this. This only confirmed, as if I needed confirmation, that one never knows what the future holds or what further madness politicians will bring on us.

I prepared for the Spanish language and citizenship exams. The latter entails knowledge of the Spanish Constitution which, I learnt, con tains an article that guarantees the right to family life. My wife is Spanish. We were married in Spain so on that reading I began to feel that perhaps, after all, I could stay. If I looked around, there are many marriages with partners who came from third countries as the UK will be when it leaves. But still there was a niggle. No one knew for certain what would happen.

2017 came with nothing resolved and I underwent two more oper-ations, to put me back together more or less in the state I was before the cancer but, of course, without the optional extra of cancer. I then discovered the existence of Bremain in Spain, a group of UK citi-zens living in Spain with the same concerns as mine and I signed up. The relief of chatting online with others in same predicament was immense and had a calming effect. My wife noticed I was getting my old spark back.

The events and shambles of the negotiations have reinforced my con-victions as a Remainer, not solely for my own benefit but also because I do care greatly for my country and consider that, on so many levels, not just trade, that Brexit will damage the country. I have children and grandchildren living in the UK and I want the best for them. I also pay taxes in the UK and would like them put to proper use. I would like to see the country, so ruptured, healed.

Today is like any other day, more worry and uncertainty which I try to banish. The sun is shining and there is snow on the mountains around our village, all very beautiful. I have just received an appointment from the hospital for a routine scan. If it shows that I am clear of cancer then I go on to annual reviews and apparently my chances of surviving will have increased dramatically. So here is hoping. The gift of granting the status quo for all UK and EU citizens can done very simply by the politicians now, without further ado, if only they had empathy and common humanity. The gift of the status quo with my cancer can only be in the hands of fate. I simply pray that we, as a family, can continue to live our lives here in Spain as we have done before the vote. It cannot be too much to ask, surely?

Alan, Spain

★★★

After spending five years in Germany and 12 in Spain, I fell in love with an Italian citizen and moved to Italy last year to be with him. We have little choice as to where to live, since his job is dependent on location, and mine isn't.

I had accumulated enough years in Spain for permanent residency and even citizenship, but I now have to start again from scratch in Italy, and won't qualify for permanent residency or citizenship before March 2019. We are expecting a child, who will be born an EU27 citizen and will have the automatic right to live in Italy – but what about me? Until I qualify for Italian citizenship – and believe me, I'll apply as soon as I'm eligible – my right to live and work in Italy is dependent on the good will of the Italian government, and the vagaries of national law.

The fact is that I will no longer be protected by EU law since I will no longer be an EU citizen, having had that citizenship and the associated rights stripped away from me as the result of an ill thought-out, undemocratically executed referendum. There are many people like me who don't fit into the typical "expat" box. Our rights – and our family lives – are at risk thanks to the planned withdrawal of the UK from the EU, and the joint report issued in December last year is not worth the paper it's written on. After all, its own preamble reiterates that "nothing is agreed until everything is agreed", and the British government simply cannot be trusted to keep its word. It's no wonder that so many of us are fearful for our futures.

Z. Adams Green, Italy

★★★

29.03.2019 will be an important date for my husband and I. Our Golden Wedding anniversary. Not a day to celebrate for us as it is also the day we will lose our citizenship of the European Union. Where will we be on that day? In England with our family, going out for a meal in a restaurant full of xenophobes celebrating 'Independence Day'? I don't think so. On the Algarve at the end of a winter stay in our little apartment? No, we will have headed north to our simple cottage in Beiras to make marmalade or help our 85-year-old widow neighbour harvest her beans. I remember telling her on that fateful day in June 2016 that Britain had voted to leave the European Union. She simply asked 'porque'? Why indeed. I am still searching for the answer.

I lie awake most nights, sometimes until I hear the first birdsong, seething over not having a referendum vote as we have been here too long, even though we pay UK tax. I worry not for us (as pensioners we are less affected than British workers in the EU 27), but for friends and family back 'home' whose lives will be immeasurably changed. I grieve at the loss of friendships which have endured for decades, now irreparably marred by blatant racist comments both verbal and shared on social media. Why do people whom I assumed to be intelligent think that Brussels is somehow responsible for non-EU migration?

When they speak of 'taking back control' how do they explain two UK houses of parliament plus three devolved assemblies? Why are they so happy for Britain to lose its considerable influence in European affairs? Why do so many expect all Portuguese to understand English here, not even having the courtesy to learn 'por favor' or 'obrigado'? Would a Portuguese émigré to the UK order food in a local restaurant in her native tongue? I don't think so. Some say 'nothing will change....we're British....they need our money'. I think they are in for a shock.

As I hover on the threshold of sleep I fear for the safety of our granddaughter, still traumatised from witnessing the immediate aftermath of the terrorist attack on London Bridge. Will she soon face a second threat from the IRA as the Irish Border issue seems insoluble without destroying the peace process? Indeed, is her City job safe as so many London firms look set to migrate to the EU 27 if there is a 'hard' Brexit?

Will Scotland leave the Union to stay in the EU? Will there be a hard border? By now I am becoming paranoid, wide awake again. It is too late to sleep. I think I will make a cup of tea.

Wendy, Portugal

★★★

I am an older father, now 71, with a second family of two children, 7 and 9. Both spent their entire lives in Spain up to the age of 5 and 6, attending local state-funded kindergarten which they thoroughly enjoyed. When they went to live in the UK both won prizes in their respective years in the FIRST term at UK primary school.

But my story concerns the youngest, Charlie, who was diagnosed with a very rare kidney disease, ARPKD, when he was two. The disease generates multiple cysts in the kidneys, causing them to compensate for loss of function by growing bigger until there is no room for them and they fail. This means that he will certainly require a kidney transplant at some indeterminate time in the future. He may also require a new liver.

His treatment under the Spanish health system was impeccable. As a child all treatment was free and we received heavily subsidised medication which brought the disease under as much control as can be expected. He was also tissue-matched and registered within the system as likely to require transplants. Spain has a specialist unit in Cordoba for child transplants.

His status remains, even though he has returned to the UK and, of course, as an EU citizen, he could return at any time and take up any offers of a transplant the Spanish system might. That option would disappear if the UK leaves the EU and he loses his EU citizenship.

He is, of course, receiving care in the UK and indeed will be eligible for transplant within the NHS as and when it becomes necessary. However the loss of his "second chance" within Spain could seriously extend any period he needs to be on dialysis whilst waiting for a donor, and thus impinge both his ability to live a normal life and his chances of survival.

John Richards, Alpujurras, Spain

★★★

After 5 years of careful research and planning, my husband Andrew and I bought our farm in 2014 and moved to the Charente permanently in 2015. We are not risk takers, we are not reckless – we read, asked questions, joined forums, took advice and wrote lengthy and detailed business plans.

We started our business, a residential and research astronomy centre, after more than a year of searching for the right property, followed by both physically grafting on the renovation for 9 months. We welcomed our first guests in Jan of 2016 and set about building up our business.

Our careful research had led us to buy close to an airport well serviced from UK airports as most of our guests would fly in for short *astro* breaks. In 2017 we welcomed over 300 visitors, all as a result of our own work in marketing and promotion. We are not making a fortune but we are paying our bills and living exactly where and how we want to for the rest of our lives.

However, despite the care we had taken to protect our finances and our future, and after working incredibly hard, just 12 months from the day we moved over, the rug was pulled from under our feet. Yes of course we voted remain as did all our children and through no choice of ours, we have had 20 months of distress and worry. So much so that I have developed a life-changing auto immune disease, with an unknown prognosis. Now we have no idea what will happen next year. We are particularly worried that the flights will stop and our business will grind to a halt. 75% of our guests fly over for 3 or 4 nights and we provide a minibus transfer service for the airport. We have all the equipment here in the astronomy centre making it possible for people to enjoy a trip several times a year.

We are looking at making some changes to protect ourselves, selling one house to have a cushion of capital should our visitors dry up, putting in plans for remote observatories, developing the site to have more flexible accommodation and extending our marketing around Europe.

We are so sad and worried for our children and grandchildren and although we range between rage and anger and distress and tears, we are hopeful that it will all come to a complete stop before the autumn.

Sue Davies, France

★★★

I am a Brit exercising treaty rights in Italy. I am divorced and have two kids (twins). Their father left us when they were 8 months old and started a new life overseas. I've lived in Italy for many years, although I broke my residency to go and try to save my marriage, but it failed, and he sent us back to Italy after a year. I have brought my kids up on my own here. My son was diagnosed with autism and it's been a challenge, but things were getting easier and I was looking forward to the future.

All my friends are Italian, I work for an Italian company. I don't live a typical expat life. I don't have a British accent. I see myself as European. A European Brit. My identity has disappeared. I feel vulnerable, I feel I no longer belong anywhere. This was my home and my life.

I may not qualify for citizenship it seems; I will try, but it will take me 8-12 months to get the documents together (because I lived overseas, it's complicated). It may come too late. I might have to go through all the tests again to gain residency as a 3rd country national. Citizenship may not be an option for me. What if I lose my job in the meantime? I would no longer qualify to remain, after I had already qualified to stay here forever. My acquired rights are being taken away from me, and I was not even allowed to have a voice on the matter. What do I do if I have to return to the UK? Go on benefits, I probably wouldn't qualify... sleep on the streets? The UK already has enough homeless people.

Brexit risks my entire life and that of my kids going up in smoke. Their father could stop me from taking the kids to the UK if I have problems (they are dual nationals). It's complicated. If there is no deal, or a period of time lapses between exit and me getting a new residency permit, I could lose my job of 20 years (they cannot and will not keep me on the books if I end up in a legal limbo, it is too risky for them and I understand that).

I worry about losing my pension rights. I was looking at the possibility of early retirement and using my right to EU pension aggregation to retire. Maybe that won't happen now. Maybe I will have to work another 15 years, or maybe, even though I have worked over 30 years, I won't get a pension at all. This is what Brexit means to me.

The kids' father would probably return to Italy if I cannot stay, become the primary carer and move into my house that I have invested my life savings into. Here kids come first and it is their home; they retain the right to continue living in their/my home, even if I can't, their father would move instead, with his new wife. I could lose my home and my kids.

I have become withdrawn. I am tired of living with the uncertainty and anxiety of losing everything, my kids, my home, my job, my pension, my life basically. Everything. Uncertainty and stress is bearable for a while, but over a prolonged period it takes its toll. I no longer enjoy life, I used to be outgoing, now I long to go to bed in the evening and switch the world off.

I make no plans for the future until I know what life holds for me. I am waiting. I've been waiting for nearly two years, and every day things seem to get worse. The fear of no deal increases all the time, the fear for the future, if I have a future. What effect will it all have on my kids' future?

My mum is frail, two cancers (and she is very luckily to be alive). I always promised her that when she couldn't cope anymore she could come and live with us in Italy and I wouldn't let her go into a nursing home. I wanted her to be with family. That probably won't happen now, I guess. She voted leave. She was concerned about immigration, mostly non-EU immigration from North Africa! Things weren't clear to her. She didn't connect that I am an EU immigrant too. She didn't fully understand the issues, she now says. I will never forgive her for voting to put me in this situation, although I love her. She will have to live with that, and so will I, but my relationship with her will never ever be the same again. Brexit or no Brexit. All I want is my life back.

Anonymous, Italy

★★★

I moved to France in 1999, I have three children. I was not allowed to vote in the referendum as I had been out of the country for more than 15 years. When I arrived in France there was not the same 'accord' between the UK and France so I filled in all the papers and got a five-year carte de séjour, and when that one was up I got a new one. When the second card was up the prefecture said I didn't need to renew as the UK was part of Europe and my passport was enough to give me the right to live and work. Then Brexit. I have separated from my French husband. Now I'm absolutely shitting myself. I am so scared about the future.

I don't know where I stand. I'm off sick from work, I'm scared I'll lose my job. I don't know where I stand. Do I need to get French nationality to live and work?

Suzanne Capéran, France
★★★

I came to Germany as a soldier and fell in love, as many of us do. Years later, I have 3 grown-up children, 6 grandchildren, a house and I work in a geriatric care home as a nurse.

I must admit, when I heard about this Brexit vote, I did not take it seriously. I mean, what kind of idiot do you need to be to believe the lies and misinformation we were served at the time?

I was on duty when I found out. In fact, it was one of my patients that told me. We both laughed. This cannot be real we thought. Just last week, the same patient was in tears, she saw something on TV about Brexit, "you won't leave us", she sobbed.

I have the prospect of a liveable pension and a future watching my grandchildren grow up without fear of foodbanks and the racism they will face if forced back to the UK of today. I now have colleagues, friends, even my boss asking me to take German nationality. My children are afraid of what will happen, will their father be deported, will they be forced out. Will we all lose everything we have built up over the years, have to turn our backs on friends and end up on the dole or even homeless in a country that does not want us? We have no information and were not allowed to vote on this fiasco that will affect us more than most.

I am open-minded and have tried to get answers as to why this could have happened. We all know it's not because of borders, we always had control of our borders. It is not for a better NHS or better trade agreements, nothing stopped us from world trade within the EU. We just lose our rights to the Single Market. Not a future I want for my family.

I hear of the racism and violence in UK. This is not the country I love and served. Why are those that spread lies and misinformation not behind bars? I class it as treason. At the very least assault. We expats have been assaulted. (The *mens rea* of assault is to cause such fear or apprehension, either intentionally or recklessly). Our families will be split apart. Homes lost, careers lost.

I, my family and all the expats I know, are living in fear caused by Brexit. Our uncertain future is affecting our careers. I have not tried it but what are the chances of getting a mortgage today in Europe when no one knows if we will be here to pay it? When I go home to visit family and the graves of my parents, in a German registered car, what are the chances of being abused? I sometimes feel that the only real Brits are over here! For the first time in my life, I am seriously thinking of taking on German nationality, to protect my family and myself from my own country!

David Morgan, Germany

★★★

I am 71 years old. I studied to become a metallurgist but met my husband (British living in Belgium), and moved to Belgium in my 20s. After 6 years in Belgium, 8 years back in England, followed by 6 years in Holland, we moved back to Brussels in 1985.

I started working for the British Embassy in 1986 and, in 1989, became the Commercial Officer at the UK Permanent Representation to the EU until retiring in 2012 at the age of 66.

So here I am now – a widow with 2 British daughters in Belgium and one in the USA. I have 5 grandchildren: 2 American, 1 Belgian, 1 French and 1 French/British – dual national. Most of us are trilingual, (French/ Dutch/English), and my daughter in the States also speaks German.

I have become Belgian since Brexit but my daughters here may have problems. One is a widow with 2 small children and cannot work due to a medical condition. The other is a single mother and lost her job recently when her company closed the department so she is "on the dole" aged 47 with a 12- year-old child.

My third daughter in America wants to come back to Belgium to live near us but, as she is also British and has not lived here in Belgium for 20 years, after Brexit she may not be allowed to move back here. We talk on Skype and she has often been in tears – she's 50 and not given to shows of emotion.

The stress this Brexit fiasco is causing us is massive and our health is suffering!!

We are not rich. We have worked hard and, because of the ridiculous way the government is handling the Brexit insanity, we are constantly worried about our future.

Many people who voted leave had no idea of how the EU works. A London taxi driver once told me we should leave the EU so that we "wouldn't have to be ruled by a LOAD OF BELGIANS". And a family member in the UK said we should leave because there were Russians fighting in the streets in a town near him! When I told him Russia was not in the EU he unfriended me on Facebook!

They both got to vote in the referendum.

I was voted "highly rated Commercial Officer" by UK companies in a Daily Telegraph poll in 2006. I worked closely with the EU Commission and other Member States Representations for 23 years, so know "a bit" about the reality of how the EU works. I spent the last 26 years of my working life paying UK taxes as I was working on what is legally UK territory in Brussels but I was not allowed to vote in the 2016 referendum.

How is this fair, democratic or even sensible?

Linda Geller, Belgium

★★★

I've had my *maison* since 2004, years of saving up and planning before... I finally had ability to move permanently. Set myself up as Gardener... worked hard, felt I'd finally found my place in the world. Stress of former UK life behind me... 2013 cancer came, 2015 big house fire, 2016 another close call with pneumonia! But all this was easy to cope with... Compared to the Referendum! Sobbed for days... Been campaigning hard... But now feel disenfranchised, disregarded, exhausted. On anxiety pills finding the whole situation so stressful as I also have Asperger's and can't cope with continued uncertainty and change... Leavers seem to be so blind, Remainers have given up and capitulated... Most days it's hard just to keep going... I once wrote that "I won't let Brexit break me"... But I'm no longer sure my body will put up with more of this stress... It feels as if those of us left fighting have no voice... no one is listening... I hope to wake up and this is just a nightmare... I no longer recognise the world I grew up in... I keep picking myself up and fighting on but each time it gets so much harder... I'm good at putting on a public face fighting but underneath I'm falling apart... Sorry this is not my normal positive self... I'm just so sad... *à bientôt.*

Lin en Bretagne

★★★

We sold up in England and moved to Spain over 7 years ago. Had researched it all beforehand, regarding pensions being paid in the EU, getting regular rises like UK residents, getting our healthcare paid in Spain so OK for our old age and ongoing health problems, lower cost of living, sunshine, residency in Spain, etc. etc. We were allowed to vote in the referendum and did so via a proxy, voting to Remain. Thought it was all going swimmingly well until Brexit happened. For me it was like a thundercloud suddenly obscuring the beautiful sun. I spent a whole day crying, something I had never done before over a political decision. I felt betrayed by my own country. The dream I had had for most of my adult life, to live in Spain, seemed in ruins. I didn't understand how my country could do this, or how some of my closest and oldest friends could want to Leave.

This was swiftly followed by a collapsing pound, and less money to live on every month. Since the Brexit vote, my husband and I have lost around 100 euros each per 4 weeks. That is a lot for a pensioner! And our pensions are paid directly into our Spanish bank accounts by the government so we get bank rate, the best possible rate, on exchange. We can make it stretch, but life is not so easy as it was.

We don't want to return to the UK, and actually couldn't, as we don't have massive savings. We would be lucky to be able to afford a mobile home back in Hampshire where our families are. And we would have a poor quality of life back there compared to here in Spain. But we are worried about the future, about residency, about healthcare, about the falling pound and whether we will be able to manage, about the cost of flights to visit our families which go up all the time, again due to the exchange rate. The worst thing about it all is that it happened because people were lied to, and believed the lies, and not the truth that they called "scaremongering" and which is now coming true. I am truly worried for the future of the country I once called home, and worried for the future of my children and grandchildren. They will not have the opportunities we once had for free movement throughout Europe and to study in different countries and absorb different cultures. This is truly a backward step and cannot be in anyone's best interests.

I don't just feel British, I feel European. I am a citizen of Europe and want to stay that way. It is brutally unfair that this should be taken away from me.

Glenys Golding, Murcia, Spain

★★★

Rome is a difficult city. But living here still fills me with "Look where I am!" moments. I could choose where I lived, and had the courage, (or youthful unthinkingness), to just come. I am still here after thirty years. There are days, when I pass Circo Massimo, the strong shadows of the umbrella pines casting their blue shapes over the Palatine, the sky opens out, and I think, "Look where I am". I feel so joyful it is painful. I am at home.

I didn't even notice losing my vote in the UK. After all, I told myself, Westminster decisions no longer affect me. Why would I need a vote?

My companion of 20 years and I are not married. We were planning to travel now he's retired, and as I can work and find a job in another EU country. Why would we need to marry?

A permanent job contract here is a rare and elusive thing and it would be safer to have one, but tax returns are enough, and work is easy to find. Documents for EU citizens are a formality. Why would I need a permanent work contract?

But I had no vote. Maybe I will have problems finding work, maybe I will not be able to go to work in other European countries now, putting paid to someone else's retirement plans, maybe I won't even qualify for the new documents. It's difficult to concentrate on work, it's impossible to actually do something to protect myself, the happy plans for travelling have been pushed aside. What if I can't even stay? Every moment is dominated by a kind of fear, every plan is shelved. I can't think of the future nor enjoy the present. Somewhere inside me I even feel I am paying for something that I myself have done.

F.J.B., Italy

I met my wife when she came over to Scotland to work at the same shop I worked in. Thanks to the EU there was no need to worry about a visa or health insurance. One thing led to another, we fell in love and a few years later got married. When we found out we were having a baby we decided to move back to Germany. Ten years later the talk about Brexit had begun so I decided it made sense to get citizenship "just in case". Thanks to the EU it was possible to keep my British citizenship so it felt like I was gaining something rather than giving something up. The other new citizens from non-EU countries had to give up their passports at the ceremony – much as I love Germany it would have broken my heart to have to give up my British passport.

Now that my parents are getting older I have thought about going back to the UK to live. That would be no problem for me or for my kids, but as my wife only has a German passport we don't know how easy that would be for her. Applying for UK citizenship isn't an option now because she hasn't lived there long enough. And would she still be able to maintain her German passport too? The uncertainty really is the biggest problem. I applied to go to a meeting held by the British consulate but was turned down because there was no room! It was a two-hour drive from my home but I was prepared to go because the issue is so important. It is a shame they couldn't find a bigger room to accommodate everyone. Not being able to make any plans for the future is really frustrating for all of us.

Ever since Brexit there has been a surge in Brits applying for German citizenship. Every other Brit I know in the area has done it. The Germans tend to be very fond of Britain and the Brits – they love Harry Potter, Sherlock Holmes, tea-time, and the Queen. But they do think we are a curious folk too. The vote for Brexit is taken as a sign of this. Contrary to what some UK newspapers report, the Germans don't run Europe: they just understand it better and have embraced it much more. Having borders with nine other countries probably gives you a perspective that living on an island never will. Splendid isolation might have seemed like a good idea in the nineteenth century but in the globalized world of today it is just not an option. I just hope that the Brexit won't happen after all. My three children are half-British, half-German and all-European. I hope that they will still be able to live as free Europeans in an open Europe after March 2019.

Neil Davie, Germany

★★★

I came to live in La Linea de la Concepcion originally to take up employment in Gibraltar, which is just across the border, 10 years ago, and continued to live here after I retired because I love everything about it.

I am part of the community in La Linea, I have learned the language by talking to people because I believe being able to communicate with people is an education that has taught me so much.

Since the referendum I have lost my peace of mind and security and do not know how I would have coped with my anxieties over the future if I had not become a member of Bremain in Spain which has given me hope that Brexit is not inevitable and that I will be able to continue the life I enjoy so much. I still worry about my economic situation as I live alone and, whereas before my pension covered most things and I used the money from the sale of my flat for treats, I now have to take a considerable amount from my savings each month to supplement my pension without any treats. I do not wish to return to live in the UK because I can no longer afford to live in Spain and have to claim every benefit I would be entitled to (which I have never done before), thereby losing my independence and my dignity. It has got to the point where I work out how long my savings will last and how long I can afford to live for.

I find the healthcare here excellent and I recently had an operation and the medical attention was second to none. I had lots of tests: ultrasound, TAC scan, MRI and colonoscopy prior to the operation and beforehand I had an appointment with the surgeon to make sure I understood the procedure and to ask any questions. I have follow-up appointments with my specialist and the surgeon next month. I could not have afforded to pay for any of the treatment without reciprocal healthcare.

I have made many friends here in La Linea and after my operation when I was not allowed to shop or lift anything for 4 weeks they did my shopping, took my rubbish and recycling out to the bins and did anything else I needed. I have a dog who cannot walk due to a freak accident 2 years ago and someone came to carry her downstairs in the morning and upstairs at night and to take her out in her buggy each day so that she could move around on the grass and do her business. Now I am recovered I am often out with my dog so much longer than intended because people are coming up to me all the time to ask how I am, how the operation was and some even to say that they hadn't seen me for a while.

I love the friendliness and the way people celebrate life and particularly this week which is Holy week and in the summer when they have a week of *feria* when the shops shut early and everyone is out enjoying themselves and the ladies and children wear traditional Spanish dress, then they have the following Monday as a holiday to recover from the week of festivities! I know all my neighbours and we always have time to stop and chat whereas when I lived in London I didn't know any neighbours. Life here is so colourful; I love the walk through the daily market every Friday morning when I go to teach English on a voluntary basis to a group of senior citizens which I have been doing for 5 years. They are just the nicest people I could ever wish to meet and Friday morning is the highlight of the week. I know all the shopkeepers by name and if I ever leave my purse at home they let me have whatever I need and tell me to pay the next time, one even lends me a shopping trolley when I've bought too much shopping, in other shops not just hers.

I feel European and have never felt that I belonged anywhere the way I do here in La Linea and I do not want Brexit to change the life I have chosen which gives me tranquillity, peace of mind and contentment I have not felt before.

Sandra Stretton, Spain

★★★

I have moved around the world since I was 17, and I finally moved to Jersey from Scotland to take up a teaching post, and to enable me to be a bit closer to the country that was always foremost in my heart... France. For the next 20 years, I commuted every weekend to go 'home' to my house in Normandy, I'd spend the whole weekend renovating and then head back to Jersey on a Sunday night to work. Needless to say, it was pretty tiring, but I saw it as my 'worth it' goal... so that one day I could live full time in France, in my home there.

Stress and tiredness eventually got to me... I had a nervous breakdown when I was 55 and had to take early retirement. I now live in my home in France full-time, which is wonderful but I constantly worry about the long-term effects of Brexit, having only been here permanently for two years, despite all of my commuting weekends. I love France, speak French and am well integrated into the community here. Most of my friends are French, and the thought of having to leave France... and them... just breaks my heart.

I have no sense of British identity, and I can't understand the hatred and negativity that now seems to pervade society and the media on the other side of the channel. The thought of having to move back, when I couldn't even afford to buy there now and doubt that I'd have any rights whatsoever, having been absent for so long, just fills me with dread. I wish that British people and politicians would see us as humans, not deserters! Each of us has their own story to tell, and each of us have made sacrifices and worked hard, in different ways, to build our lives in Europe. We are not just pawns in a political game. We are humans with emotions and feelings who want to feel secure in the future we have chosen for ourselves... a future in Europe, as Europeans.

Liz Yates, France

★★★

Our Brexit story starts way back in 2006, when I lost my contract job in the City. We had just committed to renting a new house outside London and had been on our first holiday in a long time. Not good timing. Long story short, times became very hard and having had a failed company, been through divorce, and, as a result of both, lost my house, we now found ourselves financially stretched to the limit. This, of course, was then compounded by the looming credit crunch. Finding myself out of work for five months, I was forced to take the first offer made to me which was a contract position in Brussels. My background of financial markets and IT made me a perfect fit for an ambitious programme of work there, the only downside being that we needed to move out from the house we had just moved into, and up-sticks to Belgium. Not an easy decision with teenage children from my previous marriage and ageing parents in the UK, but we managed.

When the referendum was announced, like many, I did not ever believe that the UK would vote to leave. Like many, I still can't understand why the UK is leaving, with far less than 50% of the voting population wishing to do so, and with many of those who the vote impacts most being omitted from the referendum. My wife being Polish, I foolishly thought that whilst this was a tremendous disappointment to me, it would not affect me too much as the EU website clearly says that as the spouse of an EU citizen, I enjoy exactly the same rights as they do. What I didn't realise is that the small print says that those are only national rights, not EU rights. This should be made clearer, it being on the EU website, but, the law is the law. When I found out however, my heart sank.

So, here we were, June 2016, looking for houses in France. We had already lost one house owing to some weird mortgage rule so now planned to rent a house in France for 6 months whilst we looked for our dream home. In order to find this rental house, we visited for a week to select one, near to Toulouse to help my travel to work, which was by that time in Finland. It was during this trip, June 24th 2016, I woke up, made the coffee, not even thinking about the referendum as the previous evening, Remain had it by some margin. When my wife came into the kitchen and gave me the news, I felt emotions I had never experienced before and which to this day, I cannot properly describe: disbelief, betrayal, abandonment, shock, anger, all these do not even get close. I AM EUROPEAN!!! That's the way I have grown up.

So here's a funny thing. Apparently, when a country decides to do something immensely stupid, the value of their currency goes down until the exchange rate is unrecognisable. This had a massive impact on our savings, which were, of course, in pounds. I conservatively estimate it cost us a quarter of our savings. Thanks. But, as we all now know, the story does not end there. Still believing that as the spouse of an EU citizen, like the EU website says, I would enjoy all the rights of an EU national, (including freedom of movement), we decided there and then, during breakfast of 24th June 2016, to move to France irrespective and abandon the country that seemingly had just knifed us in the back. After all, we had spent the past 10 years dreaming of it. So, a month or two later, we found a wonderful house in Dordogne, which we are very lucky to now call our home.

Having recently found out that freedom of movement is not part of the deal, I now find myself worried sick, (in early to mid-50s and not exactly every prospective employer's idea of a snatch), about whether I am going to lose everything, again. If, and I mean if, freedom of movement is not included in whatever stupid deal the UK brokers with the EU, my business will be dead. There is no real small consulting / contracting business space in France, and certainly not for someone like me who tries, but struggles with the language. That leaves the UK. So as a complete irony, I may find myself forced to commute to a country I no longer feel part of, just because I was born there, a country where if there is no freedom of movement, the industry I work in will be decimated, this industry, in which I have spent the last 10 years building a network and reputation, which overnight have been declared ineligible for the markets that need my expertise, by a minority who doesn't even understand what they've done.

So where are we now? In Catholic theology, Limbo is defined as the condition of those who die in original sin without being assigned to the Hell of the Damned. Dictionary.com also describes it as "a place or state of oblivion to which persons or things are regarded as being relegated when cast aside, forgotten, past, or out of date", or "an intermediate, transitional, or midway state or place". Let's go with the last one. We have now lived in France for 18 months not knowing whether we need to satisfy some 5 year rule or might be subject to some application to stay. We have imported 2 cars (at great cost) which, who knows, we might need to export again, (doubtless at great cost again). We need to sell another UK car and replace it with a French car, not knowing if we can stay or not, and I need to shut my UK company to appease French authorities but may then have to go back to the UK to work. Currently, we're not officially entitled to healthcare in either the UK or France, although we're trying to register. Plus, if we can't stay in France at all, what happens to our house? The French property market isn't exactly booming.

I could go on. But the simple fact is that once Brexit happens, unless Freedom of Movement is included in citizens' rights, or there is some way of buying it, my life as I know it is finished and I do not know how I will pay my bills.

Julian Hensman, France

★★★

After many years of holidaying in Spain, in 1999 we bought our house in Almería province with the view of it being a holiday home but after just one year decided to live here. In 2007, we sold this house and moved to another project in a small village near Mérida in Extremadura and we are still here. We came to Spain because we could, with no restrictions, looking forward to our life as part of a Spanish community. I learned the language, albeit not very fluently but the locals understand me and I understand them.

Unfortunately, in 2015, my husband was diagnosed with Alzheimer's and life has changed dramatically. I have great support from the people in the village who know that life is rather more complicated now.

The vote to leave Europe has left me devastated. Two years after, I am still at a loss as to why this could have happened. How can these politicians, who have been elected to serve the country, so blatantly look after themselves? They care nothing about the ordinary person, only in their own selfish interests of making money and the worst thing is that the ordinary person believed them when it was obvious they were lying through their teeth.

I am still terrified of the outcome, we cannot go back to the UK as we have nothing there and if we stay here, I am not sure what will happen to us. There is still no agreement on whether we will receive health care or whether our pensions will be frozen or even if we will be allowed to stay in Europe. All this grief caused by a few politicians with big egos.

Ann Patricia Green, Spain

★★★

Utter shock and disappointed were my emotions on the day BREXIT was announced.

I have the privilege of working as a consultant with different companies across Europe, and on the morning of the results I was working with approximately 70 young professionals from UK, France, and The Netherlands.

We couldn't actually get started with the workshop because the British delegates were so upset. Their reactions were disbelief that the majority of individuals across the UK had decided that cutting themselves off from Europe, open borders, opportunities for education and jobs, trading in an open market, movement and freedom was the better option than remaining in the EU.

I watched these young, intelligent, energetic men and women that morning deflate, and my heart sank and pure anger kicked in. How could this referendum go ahead when no-one knew the consequences of BREXIT? It's devastating. My husband and I moved to the Netherlands in 2003 because we could and because we wanted the opportunity to experience living and working in a different culture. Our first son was born at the end of 2003 and we quickly made the decision that the lifestyle, quality of life for a young family, and the opportunities we saw here made for a much better place to stay and live in.

I applied to vote and didn't receive my online voting ballot and neither did many British friends. It was our right to vote and yet the system didn't work. How many other people were in our situation? Could our vote have swung the results? I went to a meeting held by the Amsterdam mayor. He told us that they would do all they could to help the British stay – wonderful news – but can the Dutch really help us?

We now feel trapped, scared that we don't have the freedom to choose where we want to live, work and bring up our family. Disbelief that we may be forced to return to a country that we don't want to go back to yet, that has changed so much since we left, that our kids don't know, a place where our children have never been educated. We don't want this, and yet feel hopeless that we can't do anything about it.

I feel trapped and pushed into deciding to give up my British citizenship to keep the life I love. Is this really the option? How can the

UK survive without an inclusive workforce? Bitterness, sadness and frustration sit at the base of my stomach – topped with hope that there will be other options.

W.M.J., Netherlands

★★★

I find this difficult to talk about because I have always held on to the knowledge that one day I would "go home" but, with the referendum, all that changed. Here is the story of my life as a European citizen.

I first moved to Italy in the late 1990s. It was a tough decision because it meant giving up on what seemed to be a quite good career. I'd qualified as a chartered accountant and had gone on to work as European financial accountant for a multinational. It was a great environment where people moved around easily between different countries to gain experience. It was in that environment that I met my future husband. He was on secondment from the Italian branch. When he was moved back to Italy, we made good use of cheap European flights and, for a year, we carried on a long distance relationship. After much thought I decided to resign and move to Italy. My accountancy qualifications weren't recognised in Italy and, at the time, I didn't speak Italian so I decided to get a TEFL qualification so I could teach English. I passed with a good mark and secured a permanent contract with a good school.

All seemed good, but then the multinational decided (almost overnight) to send my other half to the company headquarters in the US. Because we weren't married I was not able to go with him. I visited a couple of times and we decided to get married so that I could be with him. I got a job for a while in Spain, (easily as a European citizen), and saved up money for our wedding. We lived in the US for 2 years and my British–Italian–American son was born there. Unfortunately, when we returned to Italy our marriage broke down and I went through years of hell trying to move back to the UK with my son. The courts wouldn't hear of it and I had to find some way of supporting myself, (either that or return to the UK without my son which was obviously unthinkable). I set up a small business advising Italian accountants and lawyers on dealing with foreign clients and also offering specialized translations. Over the years I have built up a good reputation and now write and deliver courses to the Rome association of accountants for their accredited continued professional education.

In the meantime, I also met my current partner, (12 years ago). He spent 10 years working in the UK before I met him and it has always been our plan to return to the UK when my son finishes school in 3 years' time. This dream is what has kept me going through many difficult years. Now it appears to have been shattered.

My worry is that my Italian partner won't be able to come to the UK. There have been various promises that EU partners of British citizens will be able to move to the UK but, as we've heard many times, "nothing is agreed until everything is agreed" so it's still very much up in the air. This makes me feel very anxious and stressed because I can no longer make definite plans for my future. It's hard when what you thought was your future is snatched away from you like that.

I've gone through, in fact I'm still going through, a period which I can only describe as a kind of mourning. They say there are five stages to grief: denial, anger, bargaining, depression and acceptance. I've reached the bargaining/depression stage, but I will never reach the acceptance stage – I will never accept Brexit. I fight against it every day, I've become very active politically – going on marches and joining action groups on social media – doing everything I can to protect the rights of future generations. My son is lucky – he has two European passports and an American one as well – but his cousins in the UK face having their right of freedom to live and work in the EU taken away from them. That mustn't be allowed to happen.

Rebecca, Italy

★★★

My family and I have lived here over 10 years so qualify to apply for citizenship, but it is an expensive process and, having moved here without that requirement, I don't see why we should have to do that. In addition, dual nationality is not an option offered to UK citizens in Spain and so, if we have to give up our UK passports, I am not sure what the implications would be, e.g. on reaching pension age, will we be able to claim our UK pensions that we have paid into over the years?

I now live in a state of insecurity with a whole jumble of emotions. I have felt bereaved, worried, frustrated, angry, betrayed, unsettled, tearful and ashamed, especially on reading how EU citizens in the UK are being treated. What has happened to the country I thought I knew?

Yvonne, Spain

★★★

We never planned to stay in Brussels but almost 10 years on, we're still here. My business took off, we got married, my husband took a different job with another law firm, we bought a house and eventually had a baby.

Brussels is a funny place: it's two-thirds non-Belgian and the variety of languages spoken and cultures that you come across can make it hard to feel that you're actually in one country. Having a child here has definitely made me feel rooted in the Belgium…not just the cosmopolitan bubble.

Our son is now four and goes to a French-speaking Belgian school 5 minutes from our house. He is bilingual, has friends from all over the place including Belgium, France, Spain, Brazil and Bulgaria and he has never known anything different.

Difference – whether it's of country, language, or skin colour – is something he's completely at ease with and I will always be grateful for that.

As for myself – I have never felt as at home anywhere as I do in Brussels.

It just feels right.

Brexit poses all sorts of challenges for us. We're less worried about the residency issue than the work one. At the time of writing the negotiations are still ongoing and there are still outstanding questions about the recognition of my husband's legal qualifications outside Belgium.

In my case, my business is reliant on free movement and the ability to travel easily in Europe. To date I've travelled to work in 20 European countries and I'm sure that the lack of paperwork is one of the reasons I get the offers.

I have some big questions about working in Europe after Brexit.

Will Brexit mean I'll need to get work permits in 26 countries? How much will this cost a small business owner? And will my clients still think I'm worth it?

We're starting the process of applying for Belgian citizenship. We anticipate that it will be fine but you have to have all your ducks lined up and there's no guarantee of a positive outcome. But I'm hopeful we'll get it, not just because it means we get to keep our precious right of free movement but also because it feels like a conscious decision to reaffirm our love of Europe at a time when there is so much upheaval.

Laura Shields, Belgium

★★★

I'm a British woman living in France. I moved from Britain to Ireland with my husband in 1990. There we had four children who, fortunately, all have Irish nationality. We moved to France in 2001.

The children were then aged 9, 8, 6 and 4. We soon settled in and started a building business. I improved my French and became involved with the parent-teacher organisation. We got 10-year *Cartes de Séjour*, confirming our right to live and work in France.

In 2007 we were divorced. I was offered three jobs, took one and worked until 2009 when I was made redundant. By this time, work had become harder to find, so I joined a wonderful French cooperative that allowed people to work on a trial basis before committing themselves to starting a business.

I registered as a translator and interpreter in 2012. My *Carte de Séjour* ran out the same year, but when I went to the prefecture to renew it I was told that they no longer issued them "because EU citizens don't need them".

Little did they know what would happen just four years later!

I began by helping people moving to France and then started working for companies too. I now have clients from France, UK, Ireland, Holland, Germany, Belgium and Slovenia. I also translate academic papers for universities.

Freedom of Movement is very important to me and I feel devastated at the thought of losing it, but if I also lost right to work for EU clients, my income would plummet. So far for 2018 it would be down by over 90%! I couldn't change my client base quickly enough to survive this. I would have to sell our family home. And at 56, in a rural area with about 15% unemployment, I'm never realistically going to find another permanent job.

My partner and his children are French. I'm involved in a local sustainable development and environmental educational associations. My entire family is 'well integrated' into French society.

So where am I now?

As the only Brit in the family I remain very worried about the future.

Hopefully I'll have the right to stay, but I also need the right to continue to work in Europe and to work for EU clients.

I'm considering applying for French nationality or a 10-year residence card but am afraid of being turned down because I don't quite meet the income criteria. A refusal can mean having to leave the country and I dare not take that risk. There is also a permanent residence card, but it's only open to those whose existing ten-year card is due for renewal, and I don't have one since the prefecture refused to issue it!

I feel powerless. I await the results of the negotiations to learn my fate.

The uncertainty keeps me awake at night. My life is 'on hold'. Many of us who have been living happily in Europe for many years still don't know we will stand.

H.T., France

★★★

I have lived and worked in Spain for 30 years. We came here as a family before Spain joined the EU and so have lived through a time of great change here. My four children were brought up and educated here and three of them have moved to UK, two to study and my eldest is working there. My eldest son has met a Spanish girl who has worked in the UK as an NHS dentist for the past 10 years. They have decided to leave, especially after Brexit, and bring their children up in Spain.

I have a business in Spain in health care, which was established in 2000, catering mainly for the expat community. Many of my clients are very worried about the effects of Brexit on their pensions and health care arrangements. Some have already sold up and left, their dreams shattered. As a business, I import goods from UK and this will stop if Britain leaves the EU.

I am concerned for my business and its future here. I am concerned for my children and grandchildren and how my family could be divided by Britain leaving the EU. My mother is Irish and I hold an Irish passport so, if necessary, I could change nationality. I also remember the seventies, pre-EU; when we had constant bomb scares, strikes, power cuts and a 3-day week. I do not want to return to that scenario! My grandfather was from Northern Ireland and my grandmother from Eire. To enforce a border there would be a disaster and so I worry about that and I don't see a solution.

I was not allowed to vote and neither was my daughter-in-law, as an EU citizen living in UK. This I see as an infringement of our human rights. We stand to lose our jobs, homes and way of life without a vote. Up to now, we could transfer our pensions from UK to another European country in order to make up the years needed to gain a pension. What will happen now? What will happen as regards travel, flights etc.? No-one can give us answers.

There also seems to be very little dialogue about Gibraltar. In the area where I live and work, many of my clients live in Spain and work in Gibraltar. What will happen? The Gibraltarians were allowed to vote and they voted to Remain. Why were we denied the right to vote?

After the referendum, I felt sick and depressed. Our lives had been disrupted and we had no say in it. No-one can give us assurances of the aftermath of Brexit but up to now the pound has fallen on the world market, jobs are being lost in international companies moving out of UK, and services are diminishing as European workers are leaving. Our freedom of movement and freedom of education within Europe is threatened and we can do nothing.

J.S.M., Spain

PART IV

"I am no longer angry: I am furious!"

It's the little things.

I used to love listening to Radio 4 – The World at One, the exquisite Eddie Mair on PM. I can't listen to those programmes any more – they get me spitting expletives at the radio.

That's another thing – I never used to swear. Now, if I catch some disingenuous nonsense, I involuntarily start dropping the c bomb.

The little things.

Back in London, if I heard an Eastern European accent in a café or restaurant, I'd ask the speaker where they were from, flattering myself I could identify a Romanian from their English. Now I hesitate to enquire: they might suspect my motives, worry that I'm asking because I'm going to tell them to go back where they came from.

Little things.

In Romania, when someone found out I was British, they'd react positively. They'd say that they'd always wanted to visit London, or talk about a trip they'd enjoyed, or say "tea at 5 o'clock", or comment on our nice manners, or mention a British football team they follow. I hadn't done anything to earn "Britishness", but it was nice. Now they mention Brexit. They're baffled, and sad. So am I.

It's the little things.
But it's also the big things.

Will my partner now be able to come and live in the UK, should we decide to move back and raise our children there? Will that decision still be ours to make? Or has our future been taken out of our hands? Will I be able to continue living in Romania? Will our family be torn apart on the altar of Johnson's cavalier egomania and opportunism, Farage's jingoism, May's obtuseness, David Cameron's recklessness, our political class's cowardice, a third of the populace's xenophobia, a lie on a bus?

The big things.

Will my country even continue to exist in its present form? Will Scottish independents pull off what they didn't quite manage to do a few years ago? Will that encourage Northern Ireland and the Welsh to follow suit? Will we see the Balkanisation of the UK?

Big things.

Will foreigners feel safe in Britain? Or will racists seize the momentum, emboldened by what they see as the defeat of political correctness and liberalism? Will workers lose their jobs, as companies pull out of an inward-looking, declining island nation? Or lose their rights, as protective, sensible EU laws are jettisoned to gratify the wealthy and powerful?

Will my sons' generation enjoy the same opportunities that we've had – the travel and togetherness, the cultural and social exchanges, the friendships and relationships? Or will all that discovery now be rendered off-limits, bureaucratic, burdensome?

It is so many things, little and big, every day. It's a collective blindness and insanity, and I will do all that I can to rouse our nation from its stupor.

Anonymous, Romania

★★★

WINDRUSH and BREXIT.

I'm the son of a Windrush immigrant. My father left his family and moved to the UK because, as a British citizen, he was asked to come and help rebuild a post-war Britain and take on jobs that English people, at that time, didn't want to do. He and his fellow immigrants arrived with high hopes of a bright future. Instead they found a country that was cold and citizens that were, for the large part, hostile. My father and his fellow immigrants lived in the cheapest housing, often overcharged by unscrupulous landlords because of their colour; it was all they could afford, and anyway, many landlords refused to rent out to "niggers", "sambos", "spades" or "darkies". I still remember signs landlords used to put up in their windows stating: "NO IRISH, NO BLACKS, NO DOGS". They put up with being ignored in queues, treated as second class citizens at work, and being beaten up or simply spat at on the street. My father would phone to ask about rooms to rent, he'd be informed that there were plenty available, only to turn up on the doorstep to be told that the rooms had all been 'miraculously' rented.

As a youngster I listened to my father's friends discuss the trials and tribulations they went through. They had a far from pleasant time. My father couldn't afford shampoo and washed his hair with Daz for months after his arrival, the same detergent he used to wash his clothes – it was all he could afford. Friends of his sometimes had to eat tinned cat or dog food because it was cheaper than the human equivalent. Of course, there were exceptions – I remember instances of warmth and kindness from some non-blacks. Thankfully, not everybody was prejudiced.

Like most Caribbean immigrants, my father intended to make some money and go back home to his family. However, life got in the way. People married, had children and made a life in the UK. As they grew older, family members back home passed away until, as in my father's case, there was nobody left to go back home to.

My father committed a worse crime, he married a white woman! Walking down the street with his white Spanish wife was not easy to say the least. However, they stoically put up with the whispered and shouted insults. Their sons, of course, were "half-caste" who were regularly stopped and searched by the police, followed by store detectives in supermarkets or barely tolerated by white neighbours; that is until they were seen holding said neighbour's daughter's hand. Some of our white friends' parents would not allow us reciprocal visits to our friends' houses, despite professing that they had loads of 'coloured' friends! It is no surprise, therefore, that whilst Caribbean immigrants were generally law-abiding citizens whose nature was friendly and outgoing, many of their children's attitudes to the world around them were shaped by the hostile environment they grew up in.

My parents worked hard for over 40 years and decided to move to Spain for their well-deserved retirement.

They found peace there, as well as the warmer climes they had left behind.

In 2016, their world was turned upside down by the Brexit referendum result. Suddenly they were, as the Prime Minister said, "citizens of nowhere". Their small pension took a huge hit and at aged 86, their future and much-needed healthcare in Spain was placed under threat. A referendum in which they, who had contributed to the UK tax and social security system for a combined 70 years or so, were denied a vote, having been outside the UK for over 15 years, but in which career criminals, drug pushers, murderers, rapists and people who've never seen a day's work in their life were given their say. This despite the fact that it is they, and fellow emigrants like them who'll be the most affected by Brexit − if it happens…

Windrush citizens − because that is what they are − have been treated in a despicable manner. There are committees, quangos, and study groups that consider and decide on policy before it's enacted. I do not for one minute believe that they did not consider the most important immigration event of the last century. I am convinced they simply didn't care. In the case of EU citizens, this self-centred, blasé indifference towards their rights shames Britain and its citizens.

The irony is that should my father be forced to return to the UK because of a post-Brexit scenario in which he can no longer receive medical treatment in Spain (which by the way is of a much higher standard than the NHS), my mother would not be allowed to return, and if he were allowed back, my father would likely be one of those threatened with deportation and no health cover.

The indifference of the Government towards EU and Windrush citizens' rights, and the ignorance and self-centred attitude of many leave voters who were too short-sighted to understand many of the implications of their vote, has indeed meant that my father has become a "citizen of nowhere".

This is why I will fight Brexit to the bitter end.

Raymon Moonilall, Gibraltar

★★★

For some inexplicable reason the writing of this testimony has proved incredibly difficult. The sharing of feeling and emotions to an unknown audience I suppose is not a very British trait. So I am going to be very "Un-British" and wear my heart on my sleeve for a change. I will begin with an apology. I apologise to my parents for the horrendous argument that we had about Brexit and the different choices we made at the Referendum, I apologise for not seeing you for over a year. I apologise to my sister for not making time for her and her life, this last

18 months. I apologise to my darling friends for not being in touch as much as I normally would. This is all because I feel adrift, lost, In Limbo. It hurts very much to have your life and the right to live as you have chosen, and been legally permitted to do so, sacrificed on the altar of Brexit. I am no longer angry, I am furious; I am active, focusing my attention, by campaigning, which is a democratic right, on those really responsible for the proposed illegal removal of rights to live your life without interference from Government and State. YOU DO NOT HAVE MY CONSENT TO CHANGE OR REMOVE MY LEGALLY EXERCISED TREATY RIGHTS.

Debbie, NL

★★★

I come from what I think was once known as a working-class background – my maternal grandfather was a butcher and my dad's dad a French polisher by trade, my dad was a motor mechanic and my mum a stay-at-home parent after I was born – and I grew up on a variety of council estates in a west London suburb.

I was born in in 1958 and was fortunate enough to grow up in a household in which books were plentiful and education held in high esteem, so after going to state infant and junior schools I was fortunate enough to go to a fee-paying school with the support of a Local Education Authority grant, which meant that my parents had to pay a nominal annual contribution and I enjoyed a public-school standard education. I had a talent for languages, and eventually got a degree in French and German. Having met my soon-to-be first wife in Germany during my gap year at university, we returned to Germany after I graduated.

I've lived and worked in Germany since 1980. Although I haven't actually taken German citizenship – as a citizen of an EU member state, I always told myself, why should I? – I feel completely at home and integrated in German life and culture. I speak near-native German. My wife and my offspring are German citizens, (I am the only weirdo in our household in that I have a British passport as my sole means of identification). I am gainfully employed as an English teacher in adult education. I am a homeowner (or I would be if I had finished paying for it). I pay taxes (through the nose) in my adopted country, yet I have always maintained a considerable amount of pride in my native land, its people, its traditions, its sometimes infuriatingly insular quirkiness, its aura of continuity. If you've read 'Notes From A Small Island' or 'The Road To Little Dribbling' by Bill Bryson, you will get the general idea. Despite loving Germany and its attendant delights, I always felt that Britain was still there in the background, immutable and dependable, should I ever wish to go back.

Then came That Referendum.

I, of course, was denied a chance to vote because of my long residence outside the UK, but I said to myself: "Surely the Great British Public will not vote to leave the EU? Why should they? They've never had it so good!", to quote another great believer in European unity, the now discredited Edward Heath.

Sadly, my prophetic powers soon proved to be woefully deficient, just as they had been in the run-up to the last presidential election in the USA, where I had cheerfully believed that no country in its right mind could possibly elect The Orange One in preference to Hillary Clinton.

If I was unprepared – perhaps naively – for the result in favour of Leave, I was even less prepared for the horrifying repercussions which followed the announcement that Brexit would become reality in the not-too-distant future. The disgraceful abuse, verbal and physical, of anyone who did not appear to comply with UKIP or the BNP's idea of what a true Englishman should look or sound like; the scrawled invitations to Poles, Romanians and what have you to "Fuck off back where you came from" that were put through letterboxes or stuck behind windscreen wipers by the kind, considerate and tolerant neighbours of these unfortunates. The crowing that we, (we? We??WE??!), had "got our country back".

For me, this was the turning point. I was no longer proud to be British. How could I possibly defend a political system – I won't say a nation, because I know there are plenty of shocked Remainers in Britain – that was at least complicit, if not actually instrumental, in legitimising long-harboured xenophobia, racism and ignorance? How could I look myself in the face in the mirror and feel anything but shame and horror at the treatment of fellow humans in much the same situation as myself – guests in a foreign country – by my fellow Britons?

I could say "I'm all right, Jack – the Germans won't/can't chuck me out, I've been here too long, Germany is my adopted home, my family and life are centred here", but that is not the point. The point, for me, is that Brexit spells the end of more than 70 years of relative peace and stability in Europe, a continent seemingly divided by political borders and a diversity of languages and cultures, but united by a single market, shared prosperity through the EU, and shared common values of liberty, tolerance and common decency – not to mention freedom of movement for all European citizens. The petty dreams of grandeur dreamed by Little Englanders who do not realise that the sun really has set on the British Empire once and for all, and possess the arrogance to believe that Johnny Foreigner will come begging on his hands and knees to John Bull will, I fear, be nothing more than dreams.

At the moment, my overriding emotion at the prospect of Brexit is disbelief.

Disbelief at the bare-faced cheek of the political establishment and its sacrifice of the good of the country and its people to political expediency. Disbelief at the shameful, degrading and arrogant treatment meted out to EU citizens now living in the UK, at the uncertainty in which they, I and millions like us are now forced to live. Disbelief at the headlong rush into cultural and economic isolation that will happen after Brexit. Disbelief that I, who have lived among Germans for nearly 38 years and never – no, not once! – heard anything remotely like serious abuse of me personally, or my country generally, for being British, and have always felt welcome in this open, tolerant, sometimes infuriatingly bureaucratic, but always friendly country, now feel alienated from and ashamed of my native land. My genetic and cultural roots are deeply embedded in English soil, but now I feel that it is time to pull them up and replant them elsewhere.

I still hope against hope that the process will still be stopped and we will return to a semblance of sanity, but the damage has already been done. Britain has lost all credibility, yet DExEU's Midnight Runners still persist in their attempts to cut individual piecemeal deals with the EU member states when a perfectly good deal with all of them is already in place. Every new revelation at what doing X, Y or Z will cost after, (or even before), Brexit feels like a dagger in the heart.

I think I will apply for German citizenship this year to be on the safe side. When my nice burgundy red European Union/UK passport expires in 2026, I think I may tell HM Passport Office where it can stick its blue replacement…

Stephen Corsham, Germany

★★★

My husband and I have been living in Austria for 3 years. Although we applied (before the deadline) for an overseas postal vote in the referendum we were not sent any voting papers until the election following the referendum. We tried getting an answer from the electoral council on why we were not receiving ballot papers prior to the referendum but had no luck (just fobbed off with how busy they were). I therefore imagine we were not the only eligible overseas voters who were excluded from voting in the referendum.

I am fed up of hearing how people who have exercised their freedom of movement and are living in another EU country should just "get citizenship in that country", in Austria that is 10 years continuous residency. Austria also does not allow dual citizenship – a problem for my husband and I as we are joint British and Australian citizens with elderly parents in both the UK and Australia.

The citizenship application process for European countries is complex and costly and they were not designed for EU citizens who had little reason to apply for citizenship based on their existing freedom of movement rights. Now British people who have not built up sufficient residency to apply for citizenship in their member state are being left in limbo regarding their right to move around Europe. I work in a seasonal ski area and know of a number of Brits who work in Austria in the winter and in other European countries during the summer. There is no provision for people who are not continuously resident in one member state or who frequently work across borders. I would be willing to exchange my British citizenship for an Austrian citizenship or some kind of European citizenship alternative if that were an option. We are 12 months away from Brexit and nothing is becoming any clearer – other than we are being forgotten. It is normal here in Austria to sign a 3-year lease on an apartment rental and we are having to make costly decisions on our living arrangements without any security on our rights to live, work and travel freely around Europe. All we can do is hope for the best and that someone will start listening to us and not just more political games.

J.F. & A.F., Austria

★★★

We retired here, to Spain, a warmer, drier climate, for health reasons, we worked in UK and contributed all our working lives, raised children in UK who now contribute to UK, our state pension is paid by UK, our healthcare is paid by UK, we should, therefore, have a say for the rest of our lives in the country that totally determines our income. If you deny us a say then you should deny every state pensioner living in the UK a say; they now contribute nothing either, and they cost UK a lot more than those pensioners who live elsewhere in the EU.

P. Darby, Spain

★★★

My story started in 1995, I worked in central Poland to help build a glass factory for Pilkington glass.

I'm an Automation Engineer by profession, and was working for a British instrument manufacturing company who'd taken a contract to supply instruments and expertise, with 2 degrees in engineering, an apprenticeship served in the British Electricity supply industry and several years of practical experience, I fitted the need for expertise.

During an Easter break from work I met a girl who was to become my wife; in those days, it was not easy to "import" a Polish girl; my wife-to-be had to have an interview with the British Embassy in Warsaw to obtain a "fiancée visa" as a condition of coming to the UK. However, she was unable to work in the UK in her profession (she found work in an NHS toxicology dept.), despite having been a practising pharmacist with a Master's degree in Pharmacy. At that time many institutions had built protectionist barriers with impunity. The Royal Pharmaceutical Society, despite skill shortages, had to be pushed to accept the employment of foreign pharmacists. By 2006 largely due to pressure from the EU this had changed and 20,000 European health workers, 310 of whom were pharmacists, had been allowed in. There were even employment groups targeting health professionals in Eastern Europe for recruitment to the UK!

These changes were of no consequence to us; we, with our young daughter, had left for the first of my overseas roles.

Our daughter chose to forsake the Saudi and return to the UK to boarding school, all went well for a few years until we started to hear of "a horrible person called Nigel Farage who had some horrible ideas" in her conversation on school breaks. So BREXIT became a subject of conversation at the bar and we were shocked to hear other British "Expats" talking of how "good" an idea it was, their conversation was nothing more than jingoism, with no substance and no concept of how this was going to work in practice.

Totally lost was the concept of Britain, a strong member of Europe working to shape the world for good which had appeared to be an accepted and respected role for an ex-colonial power, and it certainly gave "Expat" Brits additional credibility in the job market; this had been true in many countries I'd worked in.

So with the end of my contract coming up we faced some life choices, where to live, and what to do, after taking a long hard look at the UK and Poland, I most identified with Poland.

Driving a Polish-registered car back and forth to the UK to clear my mother's house for eventual sale after her passing, was the final seal to the decision; the customs officials reaction to seeing a loaded Polish car at her kiosk was one of pure contempt, until I handed over my British passport and spoke to her, her look changed to surprise as I told her I was an Engineer leaving the UK for Poland.

Discussing the lecturers' strikes over 10% cuts to their pensions in universities (which I'm sympathetic to), from my daughter, and how the students are now challenging the loss of teaching hours while having to pay such high tuition fees, we question why not study in Poland, it's free here!

As the UK leaves the EU all I see is worsening conditions, but, hey, the crocuses have popped out in our field, our winter is over!

W., Poland

My sister voted leave, although we had discussed it beforehand, and I felt (feel) betrayed. I told her so and things were difficult. I have declared a truce but... how can you vote leave when your niece and brother-in-law are Italian, and you come and stay with us?! It makes me feel unwanted and I have voted not to go to Britain again unless Brexit is stopped.

J.C., Italy

★★★

Where to start my 'In Limbo' story? My partner Ange and I are both British citizens looking to leave the UK for the EU mainland because of Brexit, and are only anticipating the uncertainties others are already facing. Crude census data would bracket me as: 'British-born Asian'. To the vast number of racists who've broken cover in the wake of Brexit, this matters not a jot; my skin is brown, I am foreign, a threat, not welcome.

This thinking has very much fuelled at least part of our decision to escape the UK as fast as possible. A little dramatic for some Brits to stomach? I've been racially abused twice since the referendum – the first time since the school playground 35 years ago.

Several factors have caused my partner Ange and I to start to look for a home elsewhere in the EU; the straw breaking this particular camel's back being the UK government's disgusting treatment of EU nationals living in the UK, while similarly (and conveniently) disregarding the fate of UK nationals elsewhere in the EU. But it's endless, isn't it?

But Brexit is also very, very personal to me in terms of what it represents. I see it this way: being partly of Indian/Pakistani heritage, British Imperialism and arrogance has disrupted my family and messed with my future three times.

India's partitioning in 1947 saw an arbitrary line drawn in a hurry on a map by a British administrator, causing my family to be flung to the winds on two sides of a bloody border.

My parents were Christians and suffered sectarian abuse and prejudice in Pakistan. Dad flew fighters for the British-trained Royal Pakistan Air Force and he was promised a commission in the RAF if he relocated to the UK. He and my mum did. He didn't get the commission because the colour of his skin apparently made him unsuitable to fly jets for the RAF. You can guess the rest... signs in East London windows saying 'no blacks, no dogs, no Irish' – yes, they saw those. But, typical of their generation, they dug in for the long haul nonetheless.

Fast forward to late 70s Britain. The National Front, BNP et al. I was a pretty happy, dreamy kid growing up in multicultural North London, until my dad's (by then desk) job moved to Milton Keynes – *then* possibly the whitest, most mono-cultural place on earth – and I found myself dealing with the joys of being the first kid of colour in a rural school in Buckinghamshire. The abuse was awful from day one and the end of my academic career, as I lost interest in study and found interest in shielding my head from being kicked in. And I also found punk music – in 1978 – my saviour.

After that – things got better for a while for us 'Johnny Foreigners' I think. More people of colour on 'Eastenders', 1970s dinosaur comedians doing ridiculous West Indian accents for TV dinner audiences gave way to the right-on Ben Elton alternative types, and mucky jobs got done by foreigners so Brits didn't have to do them as much. And we all held hands through the 'Love Actually' re-enactment of the Blair years, cheered Mo Farah through the 2012 Olympics, and were thoroughly suckered into thinking we were all part of a united, switched-on, tolerant and developed society. Nope. Uh-uh.

And now Brexit. Seething, bitter concealed resentment now revealed. It's the Little Englander's revenge. Those with the most to gain from Brexit charm the most profoundly ignorant with promises of a Britain restored to mythical glories of Empire, of gunboat diplomacy, of Spitfire fighter planes loop-the-looping over bunting-draped street parties where 'freedom' from the hegemony of European dictatorship has Mr & Mrs Average Xenophobe dancing for joy. And don't worry your little heads about all that 'economic-disaster-job-losses' tosh that whiny liberal 'experts' would have you believe. Or tax havens – they don't concern you.

That this profoundly ridiculous and irrelevant narrative has been swallowed by so many in a supposedly developed nation is actually pathetic. And I'm really, really over it.

Whilst the Brexiter pitchfork and torch brigade have been conned into thinking they can enjoy their little island free of foreigners, there are of course those who would be horrified to be bracketed as racists but are as complicit in this nonsense nonetheless: the middle Englanders who just want it all to go away. I think it may be these I currently have the biggest issue with – the sheer apathy towards their own neighbours.

I think away from the economic catastrophe of Brexit, my greatest fear about it all is that I also see the current racist values pushed on news-stands at every garage forecourt becoming normalised in the way anti-Semitism was normalised for a sleepwalking population during the birth of National Socialism nearly 80 years ago. Almost unimagi-nably, this is not conspiracy theory. It's very, very real.

EU nationals, having paid taxes in the UK all their working lives, are already facing intrusive questioning and deportation. A Polish man stabbed in the neck while fishing. A Muslim woman facing disgusting online abuse because *she bakes cakes* on national TV. Gina Miller, a woman of colour (again the 'double whammy' as far as British establishment is con-cerned), facing death threats because she had the temerity to challenge the government over the legality of their steamrollering of Parliamentary process, because others lacked the courage to do so. The list goes on.

To have British people try to cheerily diminish or dismiss these impacts to my face fills me with rage.

Brexit also is also putting at risk my income as a full-time professional musician; after many years of struggle, my band's star is finally on the rise; the problem here is that we get half our tour income from touring internationally. Brexit raises the prospect of a return to work permits, visas and a costly carnet of goods on entry to a European country, making international touring much more problematic, and placing our development at risk, as it does the loyal fan base we have developed on the mainland (incidentally my band is made up of: a Yorkshire/Irishman, an Indian/Irish woman, a Bulgarian woman and me. The latter's status in the UK is at risk).

So yes, my partner Ange and I need to leave the UK as it doesn't represent our values; perhaps nowhere will completely, but I'd rather have my rights protected as an EU citizen, thanks very much.

Although we will continue to fight Brexit (it doesn't matter where we do that from), we're off to find a better way of life on the European mainland, and hopefully a better-educated, more tolerant environment.

I'm a bit bigger now than I was when I was the skinny 13 year-old being regularly beaten and abused for my colour, in a rural school playground. I am fighting/campaigning/marching against Brexit because I WILL NOT allow the bullies to win once again, for that is what this nonsense is all about to me – with a great many Brexit voters too blind to see they will be victims of this utter nonsense also.

Ange and I are aiming to live positively in a place deserving of our contribution. Bye-bye Britain. I won't look back. Better things await.

"A lie doesn't become truth, wrong doesn't become right, and evil doesn't become good, just because it's accepted by a majority" said Rick Warren, and he was spot-on.

Tim, UK

★★★

Brexit and my family history

My father is 82 years old. He was born in 1933 in Germany, a very auspicious time and place to come into the world. He spent the final months of the war hidden in a cellar as British bombs fell all around. When the Allies arrived, he defied the advice of his parents and crept out of their hiding place. He met his first British soldiers stationed in his family's garage and they gave him some sweets and taught him his first few words of English.

After the war, his own father became Mayor of the local town, Verden an der Aller in Lower Saxony. Among his credentials were the fact that his family had had a travel agent's which had helped a number of local Jews to escape the Nazis. Andreas Willmsen also became head of the local denazification committee. Had he stayed, my father would probably have completed his education and followed in his footsteps. As it was, he left Germany in 1950 after his mother took off with a British serviceman. He remembers the incredibly complex procedure he faced in trying to cross so many borders, with so many documents and visas to be obtained. Working long hours in a hotel as a kitchen assistant in Guernsey, where his mother had settled, he became gravely ill. Much to his surprise, the head chef, a Frenchman who had been imprisoned under the Nazis and who consequently hated the Germans, nursed him like he was his own son.

Within a couple of years, my grandmother and her husband found another job in Sheffield, England and moved there. My father went with them. At some point he decided to apply for British nationality. On the form he saw the question: would you be prepared to do National Service in the British Army? Perplexed, he asked his father-in-law what he should do. Tick it, was the response. They'll never take you.

They took him. For two years, first in the UK in Somerset and then in the Rhine Valley in Germany, he served in the British Army. The reception he got from his fellow soldiers was not always welcoming. He tells of having a bayonet held to his neck and repeatedly being referred to as 'that bloody Jerry'. Nevertheless, he stuck it out and was eventually offered a commission. In the meantime, his culinary skills came in handy. He was appointed personal chef to the General of the British Forces in the region. One day the stately home where he was stationed received an honoured guest: the Duke of Edinburgh, Prince Philip. The single most profound shock of my father's life came when he was introduced to the Prince. Upon being told that the chef was German, he responded to my father in perfect German. There has never been a single day in my father's life since then that he has not mentioned this experience at least six times.

His subsequent career as a chef took him to numerous countries. Wherever he went he met fellow Europeans: Dutch, French, Greeks, Portuguese. Over the years, his European identity became a central element of who he was.

In 1973 Britain joined the Common Market, and my father was overjoyed. The Little Englander mentality, with its insular and resentful attitude to the rest of the world, seemed to be on the retreat. He still has a letter he received from Prime Minister Edward Heath in response to an enthusiastic letter he had written praising Britain's foresightedness. In addition to being a convinced European, he has long been something of an Anglophile.

At the centre of my father's world view is Europe, and its institutional form in the EU. For his generation, the social and economic relationship between Germany and France was the foundation of the building of a new, stable, peaceful Europe, a guarantee that the wars of the previous centuries will not be repeated. Since the Referendum, I feel a rage that goes back to before I was born, and an ancestral fear of how the egos and the will to power of men who have simply never grown up can lead to us to mass death and destruction beyond our current imaginings. In his own time, my father's father fought in the trenches of the First World War. My dad learnt as a teenager what his own countrymen had been responsible for, and has fought throughout his life to make sense of that and to live a meaningful life in the light and dark of it. The building of European union, with all its contradictions, was an honest attempt to stop such horrors and barbarity from reoccurring. It is an attempt worth defending and fighting to improve.

Richard Willmsen, UK

★★★

We arrived here in South West France, Dave and I, on a damp morning on 7th July 2002 with a horse, a goat and four cats to start our new adventure in France. Not young, we were mid- and mid-plus fifties but still fit and able and were more than ready to start renovating the ruin we had bought the autumn before.

Over the years, we've joined in and made friends in our village and become part of French groups, entertaining and being entertained by our French friends, aware of the differences between us but enjoying all the similarities that being European has brought. Not totally complacent but definitely settled and comfortable with our new life and enjoying showing it off to our family and friends when they visited.

From time to time, we did feel somewhat surprised at the way the British Government seemed to take credit for any changes which we could see were directives or aid given by the European Government but considered this amusing if a bit dishonest. Then David

Cameron called a referendum and for me life changed on 23 June 2016. Perhaps I had been too complacent but certainly that was no longer the case. My overriding emotion was anger, and still is, that a government, by such a small majority, can make decisions which affect me, my children and my grandchildren, none of whom wanted to lose their European status. Worse, many of the people who voted to leave Europe did so as a protest against the Government and the austerity they had endured for too long, not recognising that much of the help they had received came from the very same organisation they now voted to leave!

We are now struggling to live here, the pensions we receive have diminished in monetary terms and almost certainly will continue to do so with the weakening of the pound and for what? Brexit to me is most definitely a completely no-win situation for us all.

Ann, France

★★★

I work as a software consultant in the Netherlands. I am often sent job postings from agencies or other connections in my area. With job descriptions, most of us have become used to the standard disclosure copied and pasted into it, saying "excellent communication skills and a team player" etc. However, more recently a disturbing trend has appeared in the standard disclosures in job postings: "Candidates must be EU citizens and be able to live/work across EU27 – no questions asked".

Who can blame them? Business doesn't like uncertainty. The idea of waiting until the final outcome of the UK-EU Brexit negotiations just doesn't work here. This is something that is happening right now.

For many years I have made use of rights that came from being a citizen of an EU member state, notably doing business and providing valuable services to my corporate customers in over 10 countries across Europe. This is my livelihood, it pays for my mortgage here in the Netherlands. During this time I have had two Dutch children and, of course, I need to provide food on the table for my Dutch family.

After Brexit, our rights to continue with business across borders as normal will be extinguished. Especially in small countries like the Netherlands and Luxembourg, how can you be a valuable employee or run a business with these restrictions suddenly enforced on you, especially when your competitors can continue with free movement?

As we will become land-locked after Brexit, our Dutch, Belgian, French, Spanish colleagues at work can continue as before. Being singled-out in this way, where you have worked and lived for years already, is absolutely disgraceful.

With regard to taking citizenship of another EU member state, that is a very personal decision. It should not be done as a matter of convenience to get around a problem inflicted on us by a referendum that many of us had no say on the matter.

We have truly been conned.

With the Brexit ideology still alive and kicking in the UK, and masses of people believing what newspapers tell them without question, it is now impossible for many of us to spare any more loyalty for our country of origin.

Personally, since 2016 my attitude has changed as far as far as renouncing my UK citizenship is concerned. If I had to renounce my UK citizenship in order to gain Dutch citizenship (if I could afford it), then for me, renouncing my UK citizenship would be an attraction of it, not a hindrance.

Chris, the Netherlands

★★★

As an Englishman living in Germany and denied a vote, my perspective is different to that of the Europeans in the UK, but we share similarities all the same. It's only since I've been abroad (and particularly since the dreadful vote of June 23rd) that I have come to fully appreciate just how I was subject to the drip, drip, drip brainwashing as a child and growing up in England. We were the British, victors of WW2 and by default better than everyone else. It was the Great Escape and the Dambusters every holiday on TV. I even read war comics like Victor and Commando where the Germans were the square-jawed aliens uttering robotic sayings like "Achtung, Achtung" and "Surrender, Englischer Schweinhund!" Everything we did had to be slightly different – drive on the left, imperial weights and measures, even 'Jeux Sans Frontières' on TV couldn't be translated literally (it had to be called 'It's a Knockout!' – which made no sense at all).

'The Continent' was somewhere away across the water, full of people who were inherently inferior somehow, even if it wasn't expressed directly in those terms.

Somehow, I managed to ditch most of this nonsense baggage I'd been saddled with. Marrying a German and experiencing other Europeans first-hand has taught me the truth of the situation. Empire days are long gone. We need Europe. Forty years of progress are now being thrown away. My sister and my best friend in the UK voted Leave. I don't recognise the country anymore and don't want to be associated with it now. I hate what this ridiculous Referendum has done to my country and my relationship with people who are close to me. I truly believe that future generations will condemn this period in our history in the same way that we now look back at the madness of the First World War.

G. Bower, Germany

★★★

I have loved living in the EU – 23 years in Germany working with the MoD, where our children grew up, and where our youngest was born. Then we bought a dilapidated house in France in 2002, and spent years renovating it during our holidays from Germany, and moved here permanently – we thought! – on my husband's retirement in 2009. Then the rugs were pulled from under our feet, one by one:

First, healthcare in France lost through delayed SPA (State Pensionable Age). I'm a WASPI 1950s woman.

Paying a French mortgage and ability to live on one UK pension is also impossible due to parity in the £/euro exchange rate. So – year's contract for me, living, working and renting in the UK. I struggled, but managed to keep up French mortgage repayments.

Then, SPA was delayed for three and a half years. Depressing, as by then we had already made irreversible choices.

Finally, Brexit brings our right and ability to stay in France into question.

The devaluation of our sterling pension is a constant worry. One of our children had plans for her and her husband to join us in France. We have the space for them whilst getting established as micro-entrepreneurs. They can't afford to do this at the moment, and won't be able to for some time yet. So our family reunification after Brexit is now in doubt. They may move to Austria eventually, as she speaks German, and her husband has an Austrian grandmother. But without Freedom of Movement we wouldn't be able to join them. Another huge disappointment. Another life-changing loss.

Brexit has caused rifts with friends, and caused lots of arguments, despair and unhappiness. My energies are sapped by it, at a time when I was expecting to be enjoying an active retirement.

Our depleted sterling income restricts our plans.

I'm tired of the roller-coaster of hope and despair that is the daily price of Brexit. I have not felt such deep anger, despair, even hatred, ever before in my life. And it doesn't diminish with time.

Kathryn, France

★★★

I grew up in Northern Ireland during The Troubles and, as a child, was always dreaming of peace in my homeland. I always felt that there was only one solution to appease both communities and that was through the European Union. Today's soft border and tremendous cross-border cooperation is a direct result of the fact that we are stronger being a part of something bigger. I have seen the incredible amount of EU funding which N Ireland has received and continues to do so – for now!

I moved to Spain for health reasons when I had to retire early, having lived here in the eighties. Then, I remember that I needed work permits and had to pay for healthcare. I remember the poor infrastructure and sluggish economy. Over the years, I was amazed by how this country had transformed – European Union investment alone has contributed immensely to Spain's success. My Spanish friends talk openly about being proud to be part of the EU because of this.

On the morning of June 24th 2016, I dozed with one eye on the TV and could not believe what was unfolding. The country that I left, on the surface a tolerant, open and outward looking society had made a decision to change and not for the better. What is under the surface has manifested itself in ways that I thought I would never see in the United Kingdom and it is deeply upsetting. I feel as if a cloud has been hanging over me since that day and I look forward to seeing the sun shine again.

John Moffett, Spain

★★★

Before moving to the continent, I had already figured out my general goal in life: to learn and use languages. My first summer abroad in 2008 taught me this, unleashing a burning passion for picking up new tongues. I've never looked back. I'm 28 years old now and since graduating and moving abroad in 2010, I've lived in 7 different countries.

It might seem odd that someone leads such a mobile life, blowing around from country to country, but this is how I've chosen to live, following my curiosity. I depend on my free movement rights to be able to continue my life without disruption. I have so many EU countries I'm planning to invest time living in, so many languages still on my list. There seems to be this assumption that all Brits across Europe can just gain a status wherever they are, but many of us have no built-up right to apply for permanent residency or citizenship. Staying in one country for 5+ years is out of the question for me.

For now, I'm in Norway where I temp in kindergartens but I really came here just to relax somewhat after an intense couple of years. I spent most of 2016-2017 volunteering with grass-roots humanitarian aid in Greece. The refugee crisis is out of the headlines now but even today thousands of Europeans are using their free movement rights to go to Greece and step in to provide vital services to victims of war. How could I do that in the event of a fresh crisis? How do you even get a visa for grass-roots aid work? I can say from the time we tried to organise one for a non-EU volunteer translator; it's practically impossible.

One moment has really stood out through all this. In December 2017, the EU released an FAQ sheet on citizens' rights. I read through it and freaked out. A year before, when volunteering, I had written exactly the same kind of document for asylum seekers, answering questions about refugee rights instead of citizens' rights, about international protection statuses instead of settled and permanent resident statuses. The format of the questions and the anxieties behind them were almost identical but now I was the target audience. I don't want to conflate Brits on the continent and displaced people, as we are obviously still infinitely privileged by comparison, but my change of perspective from reading that FAQ was mind-boggling. Now we're also living in uncertainty, buffeted by forces beyond our control. I try to influence things by raising awareness and lobbying our political representatives. The supportive responses I get are fantastic, but it's impossible to know if we'll ultimately be successful.

That this is even happening is a stain on the consciences of those who allowed it. They ought to give a damn about our situation. Confronting rights abuses in Greece has shown me: if you're not vigilant in defending the rights of others not to be treated like cattle, soon you might be the one on the way to market.

Owen Brown, Norway

★★★

I left the UK for Italy when I was 21. I taught English and, with a friend, began to translate Italian poetry. I have now translated 5 books from Italian – poetry and film studies – and continue to teach on a guest basis in Italian schools. I consider myself European, and my job as essentially fostering an understanding between two European nations and cultures. If we all spoke only one language we might understand each other but there would be so much less in the world to understand. Our different languages and cultures make our lives richer.

I have never been accused of being a deserter. After all, we are not at war. But wasn't that one of the reasons for the creation of the European project in the first place – to avoid war? I did not desert, betray, snub or refuse Britain. I went to live in another country in order to try to understand it. Without that how can we understand our own?

I was enraged not to have a vote in the referendum because my rights are directly impacted by the result. As far as I can see, this government has paid little attention to the rights of British citizens living in the EU, considering them a mirror-image of the rights they are willing to grant EU citizens living in the UK.

The British government has not given one moment's thought to our rights and, indeed, disenfranchised many of us in the first place. They did this claiming that after 15 years of residence abroad we have "no strong ties" with the UK, a misunderstanding of what ties are, a sweeping generalization, and entirely irrelevant in the context of a referendum that directly impacted our lives and rights in the counties in which we live.

Given this non-position and the total lack of clarity about what our rights will be after Brexit, I have decided to apply for Italian citizenship. This seems the only way to retain my rights as an EU citizen. What is absurd is that I, and many others in my position, have had to take this action because of Britain's lack of interest in us – we have, in effect, been cut loose. Other UK citizens in the EU may not qualify for citizenship and several European countries do not recognize dual citizenship, so their position is more complex.

Frankly, the way things are going in these negotiations, with government ministers seeking to achieve a series of impossible objectives, the Britons in the EU, which the government has no interest in representing, will be increasingly following the path of alternative citizenship, where possible, like me.

Marcus Perryman, Italy

★★★

I was born in Leicester, a multicultural city, and brought up with an international outlook. My parents, who are both university lecturers, rented the spare rooms to their overseas students who brought their culture, language and families into our home. It was an enriching start in life, which opened up my eyes to the importance of travel, multiculturalism and cross-cultural academic collaboration.

I studied the International Baccalaureate at sixth form college, because of its diverse curriculum and interdisciplinary approach to knowledge. A natural magnet for EU and international students, my cohort came from countries across the world; sharing our experiences and cultures vastly enriched our educational development. The thought that Brexit will take away opportunities from my generation to study, work and live in the EU 27 makes me despair.

Brexit fundamentally offends everything that I value. Counter to what we should be striving to achieve in our society, Brexit will take opportunities away from the young to enjoy enriching developmental and educational experiences. It will damage our society and economy, narrow our cultural horizons and deepen inequality in the UK, hurting the already vulnerable the most. And the outrage is that it's not something we even asked for. Brexit was mis-sold as a solution to those suffering at the hands of the elites who manufactured it, and it will leave a lasting legacy of damage to the country we call our home.

The sense of outrage at the injustice burns deep within me, but my hope that we can fight for a better, alternative future blazes brighter.

Madeleina Kay, UK

★★★

ENVY

To whom it may concern:

I envy you your confidence
  The UK will be OK – whatever
  There will not be suffering for many years
  It will be secure
  Unheeding the experts

I envy you your certainty
  Gut feelings are always right
  No need to study the implications

I envy you your ease of conscience
  To leave the club without paying your bill

I envy you your calm
  When organisations leave the UK

Taking thousands of jobs
And billions from the economy

I envy you your acceptance
  Knowing the UK is bleeding billions on Brexit
  While the NHS is collapsing
  While public services are sacrificed
  Health and safety jeopardized
  And sick and homeless die
  Needlessly

I envy you your hard heart
  When you see the actions of the Home Office
  Its "Hostile Environment"
  Its incitement to racial hatred
  Its deportation of individuals
  Its division of hard-working UK/EU families
  Splitting parents from children
  Forgetting EU migrants are not the problem

I envy you your lack of concern
  For the future of UK friends and relatives
  With lives in the EU
  Who migrated legally
  Many disenfranchised – silenced yet affected
  Including pensioners – contributing all their lives
  With no idea of the future

I envy you your disclaimer
  "It was the will of the people"
  Despite the vote representing only a third of the population
  Despite the cheating Leave campaign
  Despite its being advisory

I envy you your deafness
  To suffering
  And more knowledgeable voices

I envy you your silence
  As speaking out "won't do any good"
  And, of course, that is not appeasement

I envy you your inability
  To rail against injustice
  To lobby
  To protest

I envy you your sleep filled nights
  But then.......I am sure you know best

Scarlett Farrow, Spain

★★★

I am 23 years old and was born in the UK but feel fully European. This is because I have spent twelve years living, studying and working in various countries in Europe.

I would say that I always did feel more European than British; since the Referendum in 2016 I have felt betrayed by half of my country and cast out. The vehemence against and disregard I have encountered towards British Citizens living in the UK and EU, and EU Citizens living in the UK has left me with a feeling of emptiness and anger towards my home country.

In my case too it is also personal, as people that have known me for years and in some cases my entire life, decided to cast a vote to Leave the European Union, knowing that their friends and family lived there. Even when the difficulties about current and future residency (as one issue) were highlighted, they still went ahead anyway. To then say "it's going to be OK, it always is" or "I don't know what you are making a fuss about" or "it's only politics, let's not talk about politics" makes me incredibly upset. This vote was a life-changing decision for millions of people and in my case (and I am not the only one), it was made for me by other people because I did not have a vote.

The people who I have heard say: "Your life will not change that much, it will just go back to the way it was before", don't seem to understand the privileges that Freedom of Movement gives us. To go back to having visas, work visas, minimum income requirements, Non-EU level university fees, no mutual recognition of qualifications is all backward-looking not forward-thinking.

The nightmare that would be obtaining work visas! I love to work in different countries. Sometimes, the job I will be applying for will be in a different location/ country to where I would be residing: how's that going to work? It works so well at the moment. I want to see as much of the world as possible in my lifetime, and get the experience of working in different roles in international work environments. Normally, when you have a job interview or application anywhere, they ask you (and this is a determining question which can mean an immediate rejection if you don't have it): do you already have the right to work in this country, or do you need a visa?

Now if we go ahead with the massive mistake that is Brexit, it will be horrible for everyone caught up in it, which also makes me petrified to think about. I have felt ill since the vote and it has got worse as time has marched on. I want to keep living and working in Europe for a European-based international company, for the experience, and to be able to travel around the world and throughout Europe with my company, but now my future is under threat. I also swear on my life to never go back to work or live in the UK after what they have done and will do to me: why should I contribute, why should any of us British Citizens living in the EU or any European Citizens living in the UK do that? Why should we when, for people like me, it will never be home or feel like home, especially after the treatment we've had. Well, for me I will claim asylum here in the Netherlands and do anything to not go back to the UK if need be.

So what I'm trying to say is that the way I have always lived my life, and been raised, is under threat because of the poor choices made by a government and people who I mainly don't know and who also don't know me. I have never been interested in politics but now that my life and dreams may be destroyed I am, and I am also fully supportive of all the groups that campaign to protect our fundamental, acquired and, ultimately, (let's face it) our human rights. These wonderful groups are fighting for all of us, for our rights, protection and for our lives to go on the way they always have, and for us to stay in this amazing continent as we have so far. I couldn't be prouder of these people and also of how they are trying their best to help young people like me to retain a future in Europe.

My family and I haven't lived in any EU country long enough so we don't qualify for Permanent Residency or dual citizenship, so what does the future hold? Nearly two years living in limbo, it's cruel!

Molly Williams, the Netherlands (now lives in Spain)

★★★

British in France are not ordinary people. We are suffering rejection by, and at the same time bereavement for, our United Kingdom, destroyed by Brexit.

Sixty years ago my French teacher would never have seen me living in France. I fell in love with my Angevin wife nearly fifty years ago. It was just natural that our children became bilingual. Our careers in Hampshire schools saw us bring 500 children to visit France. It was natural that on retirement we would settle at my wife's family home.

Enforced retirement came early and we settled close to my wife's parents. I became a bi-national. When the possibility arose we bought a small second home in England. Following the deaths of my parents-in-law, who, unfortunately, disposed of the family home, we thought about re-creating our main home in England. BREXIT STRUCK.

Our dependence on being Europeans with free movement is a key factor in our style of life. We move at will between England and France. My wife's old blue French passports had been endorsed by British immigration with "leave to enter United Kingdom for an indefinite period" in 1971. With the inclusion of United Kingdom in the European Union there seemed no need to seek naturalisation. We have been advised by a solicitor specialising in immigration law that, 'as our permanent residence has been in France for more than five years, my wife has lost the right to residence in the UK.' Years of service to the United Kingdom plus tax payments within the UK are as of nothing.

We cannot opt to move permanently back to the UK today (with Brexit we would probably not wish to anyway), as my wife's elderly aunt is heavily dependent on us. To seek permanent residence in the UK my wife would have to meet the regulations of qualifying periods. At our age this is not an easy option. We would be unable to leave the UK for more than short periods making it difficult to visit our children and grandchildren who live in France and the USA.

Betrayal, anger and disgust are emotions that Brexit bring to the fore. Not only has the UK denied us to live our retirement in peace, it has betrayed the efforts and suffering of my parents and cousins who fought for peace in Europe (one cousin died and is buried in Normandy).

Whilst we are assured that our pension and health care will be continued by the UK in Europe, if at the end of negotiations there is no agreement for Brexit, we shall have little choice but to return to the UK. We are trapped!!! So much for previous service and loyalty! This year has been one of heightened anxiety, periods of depression, aggression from Brexit-supporting ex-friends and sympathy from our French friends.

Allen Carter, France

★★★

I grew up in the early '50s through to the late '70s.

Of course, at that time the UK was in a great state of flux, being dominated by the ever powerful unions of the time; the Coal Miners, the Power Stations and Energy companies holding the people to ransom to improve their own situation, but it was an ever increasing circle of infighting and squalor in the working classes of that time.

I decided to get out of the UK and go abroad to the Netherlands, in 1972 in the first instance for an initial period of about 5 years. My company gave me this opportunity at that time to move abroad. The year after the UK joined the so-called EEC. The 5 years became 10 and so on. I became a true European living in Holland and travelling all over Europe, Belgium, France, Germany and so on. At that time, of course, having to stop at all borders to declare what we were carrying and show our passports! My work took me to all sorts of places not only on the Continent but also to places further afield. My profession, an Industrial Ventilation Engineer, gave me the opportunity to not only travel to all other European countries, but specifically to get into the nitty gritty industries of the various countries.

I was requested to, in fact, take part in discussions during the Unification of Standards and Norms between the European members, together with my peers and also academics we discussed the differences between the standards to try and bring them all together without any discrepancies between them. This culminated in a European Norm for our and, of course, many other professions too.

My own company being pan-European gave me a grand opportunity to integrate into many other countries, learning their languages and cultures. I kept my own nationality and tried to maintain my UK influence in all that I did. I do believe that I have helped build, in my own small way, Europe into what it is today.

In 2005 I retired! I'd bought a house in Hungary, on Lake Balaton in 1997. So I decided to move there since my marriage had broken down and I was divorced in the meantime.

Imagine my 'amazement', grief and anger after the Referendum on the 23rd of June, when I'd learnt that the UK was to leave my wonderful Europa!!! I like many others was not allowed to vote in the referendum having spent 44 years from my native country of birth!! I had not really thought that the UK would actually vote to leave, after all we'd had so many years of peace and prosperity and had also so much more influence in Europe! So it hit me like a sledge hammer when it did happen. But never thought that for one moment that 'people' could really be so 'naive' as to want to leave!

Being now of an age that I have many, many years of (international) experience, I believe very much, that given the circumstances and provided we work very hard, we can turn the tide of leaving the EU. I am certainly doing my absolute best to work towards this aim. Not only for myself but for all others in my position and for the youth of the UK!

Arthur R. Rogers, Hungary

★★★

Where was I when I heard the result of the Brexit referendum? It really is our very own modern-day "where were you when you heard that JFK had been shot?" moment. I will never forget the cry of "Nooooooooooooooooooooooo!!" from my friend in the next bedroom who was staying with me that week. Thank goodness I wasn't alone to face the shock of "the people have spoken" 52% result. And so I became a shouter at the TV/ radio – "But, but, I´m a British person and I didn't get to ★★★★★★ vote!" (the 15 year rule prevents that small detail of democracy but the Overseas Electors Bill is moving on to committee stage so I am hopeful to regain my vote one day).

Here we go, all aboard the Brexit referendum bereavement roller-coaster – only second-class seats available as the British living in the EU27 face the prospect of becoming second-class citizens. It really is quite a ride! Don´t miss the initial stages of silent sleepwalking around in shock, bereft, carpet-pulled-from-under-me sensations, closely followed by anger, shame, depression. Next stop denial: you can stay here for as long as you like. There is plenty of sand to bury your head in. Suddenly, out of the blue, the roller-coaster shudders and hits a buffer and I woke up and found a voice.

I've been living and working in Spain for 22 years. I am British, Welsh and European in no particular order and I will fight with all my might not to become that second-class citizen in a 'global Britain' that Brexit would surely deliver. I've found a voice and nothing will shut me up.

Elspeth Williams, Spain

★★★

I saw them come, and I'll see them go

I first moved to Brussels two months before Britain joined the Common Market to take up a job connected with that. At that time, it took 12 stamps and 6 signatures to get me and my belongings legally across the frontier. Even then, the removal van was held up at the frontier for 24 hours because someone else with goods in the shipment was exporting a radio without have paid their licence fee – I had known of the risk and had smuggled my radio into Belgium under the front seat of the car. Such were the days before Schengen and the Single Market.

By that time, I had already lived as a student and young adult in France, Germany, Switzerland and the US. Since then I have added Italy (twice), Peru, New Zealand and Belgium for a second time – all the result of personal circumstances or pursuing professional opportunities not available in the UK. It was not a "life choice" not to live in the UK; I did not deliberately shake the dust of the UK from my heels. It was happenstance.

Since my first 11-year stint in Brussels, and even in other continents for various reasons, the EU has been a constant. In the meantime, Britain has become a familiar foreign country where shopkeepers look perplexed as they try to match my accent with my fumbling to produce the right change. I have even stopped making a beeline for Cadbury's fruit and nut as soon as I arrive. The distance I feel is perhaps summed up in the title of my testimony: I do not feel part of the "them" that have brought on Brexit, though without that having diminished being British being part of my DNA. Being British was tucked neatly inside being European. Now I have to come to terms with an emotional dichotomy.

At a practical level, Brexit is shattering assumptions I have based my life on for well over forty years, about freedom of movement, cumulative social security and health rights, recognition of my UK driving licence, (exchanged very easily for a Belgian one some years ago). It had never even crossed my mind that I would need to take steps to protect myself should I return to the UK destitute to ensure I can pass the habitual residence test to qualify for certain benefits (after three months). It may be an unlikely scenario in my case, but discovering it was a possibility felt like a slap in the face.

I am, of course, one of the lucky ones. If I am campaigning for citizens' rights, it is out of concern for the children and grandchildren of my friends, since I have none of my own. And I have been able to become Belgian, a move not just opportunistic given how long I have lived in Belgium overall (longer than in the UK). But without Brexit, I would probably just have gone on talking about it and never doing it. Now my Belgian passport is one of my proudest possessions, not just for the rights it brings but because it entrenches my feeling of being a European.

Marion Bywater, Belgium

★★★

For years I'd happily shared my life out between France, England, and travelling. I'd met a Frenchman, with whom I spent an important part of my life; I kept my house in Norwich, where I was involved with the theatre and worked as a freelance journalist. And I spent a lot of time travelling.

2016 changed all that. There was Brexit. And there was rheumatoid arthritis. Wheeled off Eurostar, stretchered in hospital in Dreux, I had a week and a half on a drip to practice my French and reconsider my future.

I decided France was too important to me to let go. I did my research; not that it's easy, when all the laws under which you operate are possibly going to change. Not that it's easy, when you're struggling to get walking again. But I did my research, and I bought a house in Limousin. After that, I moved my business here, too.

I'm still bloody angry about Brexit. There are days that I think bugger Britain, nasty xenophobic little island that deserves what it gets, and there are days that I just feel sad at the waste of a country that's turning its back on the world. I worked for years in economics and investment – I don't see leaving the customs union as anything other than a disaster.

Profound uncertainties still remain about the position of British citizens with under five years' residence in France. I wonder if my relatively low income will be enough to prove I'm not a drain on the resources of the French state. I spend far too much time trying to get paperwork sorted out.

There are days I wish I was speaking a language in which I can communicate elegantly and with precision, not one in which I tread like an elephant on all the grammatical rules. And I'm still fighting the good fight writing to MPs and tweeting to try to salvage whatever can be salvaged from the god-almighty mess of Brexit. But I have, like Pascal, made a bet. I just hope it turns out to be the right one.

Andrea Kirkby, France

★★★

I am a child of Global Britain. I was born overseas, "returned home" when I was three, and then ended up going to school in Germany and the United States when my father's work took him there later on (interesting to be the only British child in an American history class studying the American Revolutionary War!).

As an adult, I worked at schools and then universities in Australia, Papua New Guinea, and Japan. Now in semi-retirement, I'm affiliated with an Australian university but am in Germany as a visiting professor at least once a year. I have a second home in Portugal, where I had hoped to end up living full time when semi-retirement turns into full time retirement.

I'm told that "citizens of the world" are "citizens of nowhere". How is that compatible with the idea of Global Britain? Global Britain is a centuries-old idea. My older relatives in Britain have souvenirs from a sailor relative who was in Japan in the 1800s, and photos from members of my family who fought in Sudan and France more than a century ago. Wherever I have lived or travelled, I've come across other children of Global Britain, global citizens, persons who are far more consciously aware of being British than persons who have never had to reflect on what being British is.

We teach English, sell British products, promote British services, and on a daily basis perform little acts of person-to-person diplomacy that give a human face to the words "United Kingdom".

I'm also a European, proud to be a citizen of a Union that has helped transform one of the world's most warlike regions to one that is an example of peace and cooperation. My European citizenship allows me to take up a visiting professorship in Germany with no more red tape than a colleague from Berlin or Munich. Being a citizen of the EU has also allowed me to plan a retirement on my limited pension from Asia in affordable and sunny Portugal and still have money for the occasional trip to London for a week of theatre and family reunions.

Until now.

I know my work stints in Germany are appreciated there, but I wonder if they are appreciated so much that people will go through the bureaucracy necessary to sponsor me for a temporary work visa. I do know I don't see as many American or Australian people at German universities as I now do Brits. And talking with Chinese and Ukrainians wanting to retire in Portugal, I know it is possible for non-EU citizens to retire there, but not as easy as it now is for British persons today, who can go in and out of the country for as long as they want, with not much more bureaucracy than someone going from Belfast to Edinburgh.

People with no experience of international living are making decisions that directly affect my ability to work and the plans for retirement that I have been making. In another year, my ability to work or retire anywhere across Europe will be no better than that of a third country national.

Global Britain indeed.

Craig Alan Volker, Australia/Portugal

★★★

No one knows what it will be like to live outside the EU in the future. Nobody! I'm just about old enough to remember what it was like before the UK joined the EEC. I remember my family didn't have money, our back garden was a vegetable patch, my dad kept chickens and rabbits for meat and eggs, there was no central heating in our house, in winter the net curtains would freeze to the windows and my mum would get up in the dark to light the fire in the mornings so at least one room was warm in the house for my brother and me. My father was a window cleaner, the money he earned in a day fed us that day and some put away for the bills, we even had a rented TV that has a slot machine at the back, and when the money run out, if there wasn't shilling to stick in the slot, you'd had it! I remember going to jumble sales with my mum and nan, where we got most of our shoes and clothes, other than the ones my mum and nan made, or spent hours knitting. To say that life was a lot different back then is an understatement. And I can understand why the UK was known as the poor man of Europe back then before 1973, because life was hard for those who didn't have anything.

It wasn't until the UK joined Europe that life began to change, life got easier; for many people, the standard of living and life noticeably improved in a relatively short space of time. So, maybe for me personally, it was the thought of having to live again like it was in the '60s that I voted Remain. I wouldn't want that life for my children and grand-children. I don't want them to have to go without any more than they already do. I still believe that it has been the lackadaisical, self-serving British government that has screwed us, which sold off infrastructure and failed to invest in any aspect for 'Britain Public' over the past years, that have caused the problems in our country, not the EU... Britain should have been managed properly, and reformed in the best interest of the British people years ago, and by leaving the EU it is not going to fix anything...

Julie Ivory, UK

★★★

I remember so clearly the 24th June 2016 as if it was yesterday. I had had a sleepover with two of my French friends, we had slept outside in a tent and were woken early by a storm coming in. As we sat eating our breakfast, we watched the news and watched the results come in. When the end results came in, I remember staring at the TV screen in a state of shock. I could not believe my eyes, I could not believe that a country that was my homeland, a country that I visited often to see family and friends, had voted out of the EU. I remember also looking at my friends then my mum and wondering what this meant for my life here in France. I had never imagined in a million years that Great Britain would want Brexit. But since that day, I have come to fully understand one of the reasons why Brexit was voted in and this confirmed it even more when I came back to the UK for the first time since Brexit.

The British population were fed a pack of lies by all parties, especially one that I will not mention who later said that the wording on their bus was not approved by their leader. Then why was it on the bus? Also, on the voting paper, it said that this referendum was ADVISORY yet as soon as the votes were in, the government decided to make it legal. Now this is not constitutional let alone legal. Throughout the Brexit campaign and still today, the main "reason" for Brexit used by politicians is immigration. Yet, how do you think the other EU countries work and cope? All I can say without getting angry is that it is NOT the EU's fault for what had happened pre-Brexit but the British Government's fault.

The British in Europe are bargaining chips, we are pieces of a poker game that the British Government think they can play with. I have never ever been scared in the nearly 13 years I have lived in France about my life here apart from when Brexit happened and when the French presidential elections happened. Today, 20 months on, with still no clue what will happen, I am struggling to decide on a future, on a Master's degree. I am IN LIMBO.

To the British population, to the British government, if you happen to come across this, listen to the song by P!nk called "What About Us", because this is a song that resonates with me, that has the words I would love to tell the PM and the British Government. Because what about us in limbo due to your mistakes and your lies?! What about us that you so happen to forget about during your speeches? None of us are going to be your bargaining chips.

Beth, France

★★★

The life I have spent years striving to build in Spain depends utterly on my being able to continue to reside and work here, and to get healthcare and pension. However, all of that is now fraught with uncertainty due to Brexit, and at this stage of the game I don't really have anywhere else to go.

I first moved to Spain ten years ago, (in 2008), when my then employers posted me here after years of traipsing around the world as a correspondent; then in 2012, I decided to stay and try to go it alone as a freelancer. This was a tough decision because as a freelancer you literally never know where your next penny is coming from and spend half your life chasing people who owe you money.

However, the skill set and contacts I'd built up suited me far more to staying here than moving on yet again, and as an EU citizen, at least I didn't have to worry about work permits, residency visas, or healthcare. Furthermore, I could benefit from all sorts of additional bilateral agreements covering everything from pension contributions to driving licences.

As I was also planning for the long term, in 2015 I took the plunge and bought a flat, in the expectation that I could work and pay for it as an EU citizen. Just 18 months later came the EU referendum and as things stand, I shall no longer be an EU citizen in March 2019, just a year after the time of writing.

No one can really say what comes next, because no final agreement has been struck and even when – or if – that happens, no one knows how it will work in practice. As someone who earns too little to pay "full stamp" (social security contributions on a permanent basis), I have already had administrative problems with residency and health-care, so cannot be overly optimistic about the future.

Let me also say I am sorry I wasn't given a choice in the matter, because Britain's laws deprived me of a vote – the most basic democratic right there is – merely due to my having spent more than 20 years out of the country. As well as unfair, because I am no less of a citizen merely because I live abroad, it was absurd for it put me and millions of others on a par with convicts and some (but not all!) certified lunatics. While I understand that this will soon be rectified, it'll come too late to help us.

Returning to Britain is not a practical option either, because I haven't worked there since 1986 and the industry I worked in is now long gone. The job market is bad enough when you are in your mid-fifties (like me), and that is no time for starting from scratch, anywhere, so I need to hang on to what little I have. To put it another way, I would most likely only be burden were I forced to return to my land of birth and citizenship, love it though I surely do.

Besides, I should like to be the judge of where I live, and in my case it took a long, hard slog to get here, from the shop floor in St. Helens via reporting on guerrilla wars in Mexico, with two or three career changes and residing in seven different countries on the way, after which I decided it was time to settle down.

Let me also say I have grown very fond of Spain, having travelled the length and breadth of it as a correspondent, as well as a keen cyclist, and have soaked up its culture as an avid reader, literary translator, and cinema and theatre goer, not to mention just chatting to all comers in cafés.

Now, I had been mulling over applying for Spanish citizenship for a while, as it is a logical step to take for anyone who comes to a country to stay, especially one who has "gone native" in just about every respect. What made me hesitate was the thought of renouncing my British nationality, but since the referendum I have been counting the days until I qualify to apply. After that, I will have to wait for maybe years and thus face yet more uncertainty.

Be that as it may, I am heartened by the way every Spaniard I have spoken to about my application has encouraged me.

Of course, I shall always be very attached to Britain, where all my family still live as well as my oldest friends.

Even today, tears well up in my eyes when I hear "You'll never walk alone", and I feel like kissing the ground when I land at John Lennon Airport, before flinging my arms around my waiting relatives, then gathering with old friends in old haunts.

But that doesn't put bread on the table, and neither did it back when I first decided to leave at a time of mass unemployment in the grim 1980s. All I ask is to be able to continue to work and pay my way in life, as I always have done, or in legal language to have my acquired rights respected. It's in everyone's interest and shouldn't be too much to ask for.

Martin Roberts, Spain

★★★

Having a Romanian wife and a 2-year-old son with dual citizenship I understand that it is unlikely that we will be split up, however severe Brexit is. What scares me is the incompetence, insincerity and flippancy of the government that I still vote for and which is supposed to represent my best interests.

I believe that Brexit has been hijacked by those who stand to gain the most from it, that it is legitimising racism on a scale not seen for a generation, that it will cause a crippling shortage of NHS workers, and that it will result in a downward slide in social mobility in the UK that is outright dangerous.

Let me hone in on a particular bit of flippancy recently that has angered me greatly. Boris Johnson made headlines trying to alleviate Remainers' concerns by saying that we will still be able to go on "cheapo flights to stag parties in ancient cities".

For my family, the availability of low cost flights to the UK is the difference between my son's grandparents being able to see him grow up or not. It is that simple.

I feel abandoned. I get the feeling that Brits living in Europe are of no interest whatsoever to the politicians back home. I'm worried for my son's future ability to study in a UK university, and that it will downgrade my relationships with all my friends and family back in the UK who can currently come over here with ease.

Daniel Patrick Cohen, Romania

★★★

For me 'home' is where the heart is and in my case my heart is with my beloved wife and son, which happens to be here in Amsterdam. We are here for entirely very personal reasons, nothing to do with Brexit or that Holland is better than England. It's not surprising that as the world becomes ever more inclusive, so international marriages like mine are going to become more common as are mixed race offspring like my son. It follows that families may not always live in their country of birth.

I am not ashamed to be English. I have family and friends in the UK whom I love dearly and could never feel ashamed of them. I stood and sang the national anthem when I watched the recent rugby match between England and Scotland which was shown live on TV here in Holland.

However, I do feel totally betrayed by the UK government and I feel ashamed of ministers in the government who claim to be acting in the best interests of the whole of the UK.

I feel so very let down by the whole Brexit vote and the way it was conducted by the UK government. Even today, some 20 months later and with £billions already spent, nobody can claim that they really know what Brexit means, where it is going to end up or what its impact is going to be on both the EU and UK.

So the government handled the referendum extremely badly and left me feeling betrayed. But it now seems quite happy to abandon the millions of British subjects who, for a wide variety of reasons, now live in the EU and who do not deserve the treatment that is being forced upon them.

I worked and paid taxes in the UK for 30 years, not once have I made any claim for financial support from the state and not once have I ever been involved in any wrongdoing. My entire working career was with large UK multinationals with whom I travelled to over 60 countries, flying the flag for my country along with many colleagues who have exercised their freedom to live outside the UK, but for the UK. So why now is the UK government treating me in this way? My British son is about to start his education but we do not know what is going to be best for him because the UK government has betrayed us and not given us any assurances about our future. Rather it has hung us out to fend for ourselves, and use as pawns in their game of chess, simply because we exercised our freedom, our basic human right, to live in Holland, which, as I say, is for entirely personal reasons. I just want to live my life with my wife and son but that is being denied me by the betrayal of the UK government from whom I expected a lot more.

In the event we lose residency status, my son and I have the right of abode in the UK. However, my wife does not have UK residency status. Our dilemma, therefore, is on several levels: will she be permitted to reside in the UK *per se*? If yes, will she be separated from our son whilst her application for residency is being processed? If there is a delay we do not have the funds for a house both in UK and Holland. So if we sold in Holland to buy in UK, then we are without funds to support my wife in some sort of rental arrangement in Holland. If we delay selling in Holland then my son and I would be unable to afford rented accommodation in UK whilst having a house in Amsterdam. Will the Dutch government allow our son to remain with his mother even though his residency may be terminated? If not, then there will inevitably be the emotional trauma of a mother being separated from her young son.

If my wife is denied residency in the UK then our only remaining choice for staying as a family unit would be for her to return to China and my son and I to apply for Chinese residency as a close family member of a Chinese citizen.

A proud Brit, Amsterdam

★★★

I can clearly remember waking up the morning after the referendum and thinking my husband was having a joke when he told me the result. My reaction then was, "Well, we'll just have to leave Britain!" And so we did. We both resigned from our jobs, worked out how we could live on a small income and moved to a small house in the foothills of the Pyrenees in January 2017.

My grandfather and my father fought for a united Europe. My father served on a Free French Navy corvette. He lived to see and experience being a member of the European Community. We have both grown up being Europeans, with friends in other countries and a strong attachment to France. We have travelled freely in Europe, which has given both us and our children an appreciation of different people and cultures. I dreamed that both our children and our future grandchildren would have the same wonderful opportunities to travel and work in Europe. I still have that dream.

We refuse to relinquish our membership of a European community that we love without a fight.

Barbara Baldwin, France

★★★

Bloody anger is an emotion I absolutely share… I grew up in a mining village in post-war Britain. Both grandfathers and many great uncles went through (some didn't survive) the Great War. My father's generation repeated the experience in the Second World War. I grew up with all the myths of the Empire, and now have cousins and more distant family on four continents. I thought the country had learned the right lessons from history, in spite of the obsessive 2nd World War mythology, and that 'we' had grown out of a narrow hypocritical tribalism. I thought we embraced equalities of all kinds, had become kinder and more open, and the future direction was clear.

As a student in the '60s, I had studied European Integration, way before we joined the EEC, and understood and shared the ideals of its founders… And now I find that I was deluded about the society in which I live, that the political and economic elites did not share those values enough to fight for them. I found the wilful ignorance of, and arrogance about, the EU of our journalists and media presenters astounding, and was horrified at the ease in which others delighted in deceit and xenophobia for their own purposes. I remain appalled at the fragility − or absence − of real democracy, the lack of understanding of what a liberal constitutional democracy might actually look like, and the easy capitulation of politicians to manipulated simplistic populism.

I am depressed at the ease with which reasoned, evidence-based debate is eliminated from popular dialogue, and the ease with which party political leaderships choose to put party or personal power ahead of rational debate or national interests, or simple honesty. I find it disgraceful that EU citizens long resident were disenfranchised, that the young were disenfranchised, that UK citizens living in Europe were disenfranchised, that it's OK to be bound by a constitutionally advisory referendum with a statistically marginal outcome yet with no defined direction, regardless of whatever evidence emerges…

I am utterly dismayed that I am obliged to retain a citizenship of a state organisation that abuses its powers over human beings it determines as 'other' whilst providing a haven to many a corrupt or criminal oligarch with wealth. I resent that I have no right to retain a kind of associate EU citizenship on the whim of hateful xenophobes. I am pleased my niece and her Yorkshire husband are able to take up French citizenship, yet sad that it should be necessary, that nationality should suddenly be so significant – when history shows the boundaries of states to be transitory – even in the islands of Britain.

Above all, I rail at the power of ignorance, of false arguments, and the sheer malevolence of those who have successfully exploited these vulnerabilities for their own aggrandisement regardless of the consequences for other human beings. Personally I resent being denied the right of residence should I wish it, in any European land – my partner is German, my daughters and grandchildren live in the UK – and in a year I can expect options hitherto open to be closed. Thank you for permitting a rant. The above is only a fraction!

David Powell, UK & Germany

PART V

"I am constantly excusing myself for being British"

Why should I feel so ashamed? It takes my breath away how I have moved from feeling so proud to be a British European to the position we are in now.

Last week I broke down in tears in the supermarket here in Bucharest, initially overwhelmed by the kindness of strangers. But then the awful realisation hit me that of the many emotions I was feeling, gratitude, confusion, embarrassment at my inability to speak Romanian, the one thing I didn't feel was fear of hostility either verbal or physical, something I have never felt as a Brit in Europe. It made me feel so ashamed that I would not be able to say the same about my equivalent, the non-English-speaking Romanian woman in the supermarket queue in Britain. I put my bags down and wept with shame in the street. The enormity of that difference hit me like a sledgehammer, and hits me still. I'm crying as I write this testimony.

Sarah Pybus, Romania

★★★

I am UK born to British parents but have lived in Spain since 1976 except for a short period in London. Franco had died only months before I arrived and the transition from dictatorship to democracy was in process. I was 17 at the time so lived an extremely emotional moment in history. The Spaniards went from fear and mistrust to elation and positivism. The world was their oyster and little ol´ me was lucky enough to live through it. There was now an open window to the world for Spain. There were desperate times too, of course, living in the Basque country wasn't always a bed of roses; on the contrary, my father was threatened by ETA and actually suffered an attack. He was one of the fortunate ones. He survived. Needless to say, our time as a family living in Spain had to come to an end and we moved to Brussels. I mention this as, through manipulative politics (on all sides),

I have already had to change my life. I eventually went to London to work and study and went back to Spain, alone, 3 years later where I had been made to feel so much at home. And I'm still here, married to a wonderful Spaniard with adult Spanish children some 30 "muchos" years later.

On June 23rd, I stayed up until 4.00am. Disbelief and anxiousness was what I felt as the story of Brexit unfolded before the world. I couldn't even have a say in it! My destiny was being decided for me and the decision has changed me.

Throughout my children's childhood, I have done my best to educate them as globally-minded people, and to appreciate the richness of having two totally different cultures that complement each other. That has drastically changed. My daughter, a nurse who was working in the UK with a master in A&E and critical care, would sometimes be sent ahead of the doctor in Resuscitation to reassure family members that their beloved was now stable only to be told "We'd like to speak to a real English person please!" The month she left, 60 other nurses from the EU left with her. They were all being told to "go home" by the public and to their faces.

Beloved family relationships have also changed. On my last visit to the UK I was told by a brother-in-law that I have "no right" to a British passport and that Farage is the solution to Britain's problems. He loves my father dearly yet has put my father's health service here in Spain at risk as, if there is no agreement, he will possibly be denied health care both by the state and private insurance due to his age. My mother, who lives in the UK, believes that the A&E at her local hospital was closed "to so many immigrants" overcrowding it. "What?" I replied, "Immigrants like me and your grandchildren?" I hope she went red with shame. Of course, it wasn't true. The real reason was because they were short of staff and finance.

Here in Spain, my frustration is understood and sometimes pitied by my Spanish friends and family, yet not so much by fellow UK immigrants. I use social media a lot and I can tell you, there are UK immigrants who have voted Brexit and they tend to attack and despise me. They can´t see that they have moved to a country that belongs to the EU and become immigrants themselves. Oh, the irony!

I am no longer an expat. I am an immigrant. I can no longer be proud of Britain. I am ashamed. I am constantly excusing myself for being British. Do I want to be British? I don´t know… I know I can apply for Spanish citizenship but I have always felt so global. What do I do? How will I cope when D day arrives? I have no idea. The window to the world has closed for Britain. I am in limbo.

Sharon Price, Madrid, Spain

★★★

After the referendum took place many people were disappointed as well as confused, including me. I'm 13 years old, my father is English and I live with my mother, who is Austrian, in Linz. I currently have an English passport but due to Brexit we don't know if I'm able to keep it since in Austria you are not allowed dual nationality.

It was difficult to take it all in at the beginning and I was scared to see what the future would hold.

At the time I felt the need to change something, the need be heard and I felt like this would all make a difference. I wanted to gain attention to raising the awareness of this event, so I wrote to the president of Austria. Alexander Van der Bellen wrote back to me and I got the chance to meet him, we talked Brexit but he couldn't read the future and he explained to me that the topic was still foggy and unpredictable.

Next, I wrote to Billy Bragg, and to my surprise I got a reply, leading to another meeting. He told me how he would see the future of Britain; however, he also did not have a detailed idea of how the story will unwrap. I think the pressure of trying to make a difference had opened up a new door in me, a door I thought I never had. I think it is ironic because of something so negative, a positive has emerged.

Now, I don't know what to feel, I can't be worried because I don't yet know what to worry about. I feel like all of the past events hadn't made a difference on Brexit. I think that this vote for Brexit had ruined, in my opinion, Britain's name and for me, as a British citizen, I feel embarrassed.

Oscar Hetzinger, Austria

★★★

As I have lived in Cyprus for 25 years, I was unable to vote in the Referendum, which left me with intense feelings of frustration, regret and concern. I have two children, who are both British and Cypriot, and their futures have been affected by the Brexit decision, as has my own. I have always brought them up with a European out-look, with firm roots in the UK, through regular visits home. One will begin his studies at university in September, and the second one now has an uncertain future as he is due to come to study in 2018 (after serving his military service in Cyprus), and the university fee status has yet to be decided or confirmed – leading to uncertainty and anxiety.

In my capacity as Deputy Headmistress of an English curriculum international school in Cyprus for several years, I have assisted over 1500 EU students in applying for higher education in the UK. While in the UK, I believe that these students, in addition to the obvious economic benefit to the UK, have offered an invaluable contribution through their skills and culture. I am a firm believer in education promoting tolerance and awareness and am greatly concerned that this will be adversely affected if European students are affected by the Brexit and no longer able to come to the UK to study. Their interaction with UK students is paramount in preventing UK students from becoming isolated and insular in their outlook. After all, the essence of higher education is international by nature and Brexit-style restrictions on movements across borders will not serve this purpose. The increase in post-Brexit hate-crime is absolutely alarming.

Many of our students are now working in the UK (as EU citizens), and have fabulous careers in professions such as engineering and designing the new Crossrail system in London, or in leading banks and firms. Not to mention those who dedicate their lives to the NHS as doctors. These young people are deeply disappointed and demoralised currently.

As an 'outsider' (which I am now made to feel) looking at what is happening in the UK from a distance, I am appalled at the lack of apparent answers relating to this momentous decision. I am highly embarrassed when I answer the many daily calls I receive from anxious Cypriot parents about their children's future studies in the UK – all I can say is, "I don't know," or "It has not been confirmed." Many of these families have made great sacrifices (and of course planned many years ahead) to ensure that their children can have a top-rate UK education as it has always been held in the highest regard in Cyprus. I too have played a role in promoting this.

It is with great disappointment and sadness that I watch the TV updates daily, seeing how many people running campaigns have lied (and proved to be British 'quitters'), and this has had a dire effect on so many lives, a fact they now seem to take no responsibility for.

I feel greatly let down by my home country and deeply embarrassed and ashamed by the presentation of the UK abroad as being a country that is without leadership and without concrete plans and answers. Great Britain has always been a country that has been admired for its economic strength, organisation and efficiency. This image has now been irreparably damaged and no-one takes responsibility.

Kam Stylianou, Cyprus

★★★

Disenfranchised, betrayed. My situation is this: after completing eight years of service with the British Army I set up home in the Netherlands with my Dutch fiancée. This was back in 1987. We had two children together, the "boys" are now 24 & 26.

After the first five years resident in the Netherlands I would have been entitled to claim Dutch nationality, but I retained my British citizenship – partly out of a sense of patriotism and pride, but mainly because it didn't really matter what nationality was written in my passport, it was an EU passport and equally valid in the Netherlands as the Dutch version would've been. And so the years passed, never a thought really about nationality or citizenship – I was a citizen of Europe, with a British tag. A bit like being British/Welsh. Then this Brexit train-crash arrived.

Leading up to the referendum, I enquired online about a postal vote. To my horror, I discovered I was excluded – I had no voice. My government, the country I had served, had blackballed me from what was the most important decision of my lifetime! A massive stab in the back for millions of people, people whose lives would be more affected by Britain possibly leaving the EU than those safely tucked-up in suburban Bolton or Cheltenham.

We had been betrayed.

Then the referendum result, and the subsequent open-mouthed disbelief at what the government did with that split-decision!

Egos being promoted, reputations and personal pensions protected. Careers secured. Party interests being given far greater priority than the national interest. Promises being broken. Clear and obvious lies openly spouted. The media manipulating the masses in an impressive show of corporate/individual wealth dictating public opinion, to their own advantage. A textbook example of divide and rule. Those most likely to suffer the consequences of Brexit brainwashed into campaigning for it, defending it, fighting for it!

The country has gone quite mad.

So, after 31 years as a British migrant worker (I hate the term "Expat"), it's time to cast off my British past, I not only relinquish but openly reject my British citizenship. I am actually ashamed today to be identified with the country of my birth, the country I once proudly served.

Regardless of the outcome post-Brexit proper, before May 29th 2019, I will be Dutch.

Marty Hirst, the Netherlands

★★★

There have been three things since the referendum that have been challenging to deal with. Firstly, as a third culture kid, who was born in Germany to British parents the referendum brought about questions of identity. With one vote I felt I had lost the right to the identifier that I use to define myself... European. This is because I am neither English nor German; I am a strange unique amalgamation of both of them. With the increasingly multicultural world there are many people like me, ghosts that filter between two different cultural contexts but never 100% belonging to either. The second thing that I have had to deal with since the referendum is the increasing abuse on social media. As someone who is investigating the impact social media had on the referendum as a dissertation topic I have had to reach out to both remain and leave campaigners. The referendum has given legitimisation to aggressive and hateful discourse for something as basic as political views or ethnicity. Lastly, it has been associated with the feeling of shame for me. For so long I had associated the UK with being forward looking and it feels like we have made one massive embarrassing leap backward. The referendum has made me very much feel that why should I utilize my talent to help prop a crumbling society and economy when there are other places that are open and welcoming.

N., Germany

★★★

(living in France, writing from on holiday in Spain)

I first moved to France in 1967 as a student/au pair so you could say I have benefited from free movement all my life. However, life in both countries was very different then, both culturally and economically, so registering even as a student entailed long waits in prefectures and massive amounts of paperwork. Since then I have lived and worked in Belgium, France, parts of Africa, and, of course, the UK. I retired to France in 2007. My adult children were partially educated in France and speak French fluently.

My daughter lives in Kent and is an ICU nurse in a London teaching hospital and has two little boys at primary school. On 24 June 2016 she asked me to take the boys to school as she felt too upset to talk to the other mothers, most of whom she knew had voted to leave. I stood in the playground and listened to the reasons they gave each other for voting to leave, none of which were remotely connected to the EU.

She and her husband decided to wait and see how Brexit progressed before making a decision on their future while I returned to my village in France to watch my pension drop every month as the pound dived. The mayor and deputy have been very supportive of the British people in our commune and the leader of the council wrote a forward in the quarterly newsletter thanking the UK citizens in the area for their huge contribution to local life and expressing the wish that we would stay on despite the Brexit vote. In fact, we have always been welcomed here so how I embarrassed do we feel when contrasting this attitude with the xenophobia and outright racism in Britain, encouraged by the government and appalling right wing press.

With the NHS at breaking point, and the pressures on staff to care for patients with reducing resources, my daughter's health is suffering, the rising cost of living means she works every weekend and only sees her children after school on weekdays and her husband almost never. As a result, they have made the decision to leave the UK and will be joining me in France this year.

I came to Spain a couple of weeks ago for a break from the snow in my village! I have met lots of people here of differing nationalities, not one of whom has expressed anything but total horror at the Brexit vote and the disastrous 'negotiations' of the UK Government. The consequences for thousands of families have not been considered by our self-serving politicians or explained to the British public so here are a couple of examples.

A few days ago, I stupidly left my car and house keys on the beach wall overlooking the sea but did not discover their loss until returning home an hour later. I retraced my steps to cafés adjoining the promenade without luck and then to the wall. Under a stone was a note written in perfect French and English from a young German man advising he would hold on to my keys for a couple of hours then take them to the police. I called his mobile and he arrived with the keys and his British wife. I would like to feel similar care and kindness would be shown to other Europeans in the UK but, in the current climate, who can feel confident. I thanked them profusely and the subject turned to Brexit. They cannot move to the UK because of him and she is, as are we all, worried about her situation in Germany.

I then met another couple from Yorkshire. He told me that all the farmers he knew had voted leave and are now complaining about lack of workers and EU subsidies. He would like to move to Spain for half the year but is worried about how this would affect their children and grandchildren if free movement is removed. Yet another couple from the north-east whose son lives in the Far East told me he had married an Asian girl. He cannot return with her to the UK because she needs to earn over 30K to be acceptable. They are distraught for him.

Finally, my lovely Spanish teacher told me yesterday that his son is studying at a UK university under the Erasmus scheme and is half way through his course. He does not know if he will be allowed to finish it. This disastrous government is sowing division and fear into the lives of citizens everywhere. How can we stop this madness?

Susan Davis, France

★★★

I've lived in Romania for several years and have recently become a Romanian citizen. Fortunately Romania allows dual nationality, so there was no question of my having to give up UK citizenship, which I would never want to do. Of course, there were practical considerations, but the reason for becoming a Romanian citizen was deeper. I feel European, British and Romanian. I don't want the European part of my identity taken away.

I've felt embarrassed to be British. Brexit is so damaging and makes us look ridiculous.

Mark Percival, Romania

★★★

I stood at a door in an Edinburgh council scheme in September 2014, hoping to encourage the woman in front of me to vote yes to Scottish independence. She was apologetic, and upset. She had been looking forward to voting yes, she told me, but a team of NO campaigners had been round earlier that day, telling her that if Scotland became independent, we would be forced out of Europe and she'd be shipped straight back off home.

I told her that, in fact, the opposite was true: that the danger lay with staying in the UK, when there was already Tory talk of a referendum to leave Europe. But I didn't put my argument as forcefully as the bullies who had scared her already; I didn't want to. I felt sorry for her, being told by everyone who came to her door that her right to stay was in question.

I think about her sometimes. Two years later, she wasn't allowed to vote in the EU referendum, and she was forced to watch her worst fears come true.

And so was I, in my own home in the Netherlands. The day after the Brexit vote, I woke up stunned and utterly ashamed to be identified as

British. I wouldn't have ventured outside if I didn't have to cycle the children to school. Fellow villagers looked at me questioningly, and I told them immediately that I was Scottish and that Scotland had voted to remain. My English friends wished they had something similar to reach for, to save them from their own shame and disgust.

It was little comfort to me though, that Scotland had been scared into retreat on the question of independence, bullied like that woman at her door, only to be dragged into a man-made disaster which would punish the country for its own timidity – and its misplaced trust.

My husband is an academic, in search of a full-time job the whole time we've been married. I have long despaired that universities don't care about the effect they have on families – they expect you to drift around the world from short-term contract to short-term contract. But here we are, having followed the work to the Netherlands, wondering where the next contract will come from, and whether he'll be thrown off short-lists for being non-EU. Our already precarious life plan has been rendered a thousand times more uncertain.

Taking Dutch nationality is not an option unless you are prepared to give up your British passport (or marry a Dutch citizen). Once you make that leap, you forfeit your right to go back. It's a heartbreaking choice to be faced with.

Honestly, I would have stayed in Scotland if I could have. But we made a good life for ourselves in the Netherlands. The children have already been here for the majority of their lives. We speak fluent Dutch. I'm helping a Frisian friend learn Gaelic. That's what Europe is about to me: a positive, respectful exchange of cultures and languages, however small.

Brexit is putting an end to that. A rhetoric which glorifies the imperial English language over all others, which despises cultures it does not understand, which is mortally terrified of the Other. My dearest wish is that Scotland breaks free of that poisonous thinking and creates its own path back to Europe. I believe it will happen. I am waiting for it to happen. And that's what keeps the panic at bay.

C.B., the Netherlands

★★★

No-one has, or should feel, a single national identity. I was born British, am fond of certain British things, (cricket, steak and kidney puddings, our humour), and proud of others (our part in the early months of the last European War, the NHS), but have never been a 'patriot' in that limited sense. This is why Theresa May's dismissive 'if you believe you're a citizen of the world, you're a citizen of nowhere' at a recent Tory conference, appalled and alienated me. The Brexit vote had the same effect. It may not have been a purely xenophobic event, but rather more of a people's misdirected reaction against decades of oppression (if that's not too strong a word) by other forces than 'Brussels'. I'm even more depressed by the intolerance and sheer racism that the result of the referendum provoked, mainly on the Brexit side, and the sheer irrationality of the argument against a second democratic vote. Lastly, I've been made to feel humiliated by the reactions – usually sympathetic of the friends I've made in Sweden, where for the last 22 years I've spent half my time with my Swedish partner. I used to try to defend my country abroad; I no longer can. (Cricket they can't understand; steak-and-kidney pudding sounds revolting to them; only 'Engelsk humor' has any purchase. Thank God for Eddie Izzard).

I love Sweden just a little bit less than England, and admire her more. But I'm unwilling to move there permanently – missing the cricket, and all the rest – and Kajsa would be unhappy living in Britain all the time, for what I think are better reasons. So we live in both countries, relying on free movement between them; sharing the rights and medical services that the EU gives us access to; and – more than this – the sense of community that being in a single association gives us. I've also worked in Sweden, doing occasional lecturing, on the salary for which, (and on our shared *sommarhus*), I pay Swedish taxes. My children and grandchildren share all the delights of Sweden with me.

I may not be materially affected by Brexit – I applied for (dual) Swedish citizenship straight after Brexit, which I hope will come through soon, and which should have the added advantage of restoring the European citizenship that the Brexiteers have stolen from me. But – perhaps oddly, in view of my admitted lack of 'patriotism' – I'm more concerned about the damage that they have done to Britain's reputation in the world. For the first time I feel ashamed of being British.

I also have tremendous feelings of sympathy for other Europeans who will no longer be able to live and work in Britain, as they used to. And of course I'm worried for the British economy; though I have to say that's the least of my concerns.

Bernard Potter, Sweden

★★★

I'm not one for politics. I never have been really.

Then the Brexit referendum happened.

I have spent a lot of my life overseas, moving around with my family as a kid, due to my father's job in the oil industry. I always enjoyed this part of my life and, as a Brit living in Austria for the last 6 years, I still do. Different cultures, climates and attitudes towards life fascinate me. However, I will always consider England and, in particular, Norfolk, as my home. I wasn't born in Norfolk, but I got there as fast as I could and go back from time to time to check on the place and pick up some Marmite, Cromer crab and back bacon.

I love England, but I also love my adoptive home in Austria. Not just the kind of love where after three years I'm happy to move back to England and settle for fond memories of the place whenever I see brown Lederhosen or eat a poorly prepared Schnitzel, real love and affection for the place, the people and the way things are run here. Not only have I settled in well and been accepted, despite my struggles with the language, but my family have settled so well that we all feel most at home when we are here. Austria is our home and we don't want to leave. But can we stay after Brexit? Will we be allowed to stay in our home here and carry on as we have planned before liars convinced nearly 52% of the UK voters that leaving the EU was a good thing? I have no idea and we are only a year away from the proposed exit date thanks to a deaf PM triggering Article 50, despite the strong voices opposing it. If she had watched interviews with Joe Public on the news the day the results were announced, warning flags should have been flapping wildly in her head as she watched those who voted for Brexit replying to questions with such imbecilic statements such as "I voted to leave because I didn't think we would win" or, "I voted to leave because I don't like David Cameron". Let's not forget the classic "Yeah, well, we don't want no immigrants coming here no more, especially them Muslims. Close the borders!" I felt genuine anger towards these people. Then I went to work and the jokes from my Austrian colleagues made me feel a deep embarrassment towards my country and I came close to losing my sense of humour. We had a chance to show that we are not stupid in our decisions and we failed. Miserably.

The EU has its problems, there is no doubt about that. However, leaving an organisation which has so many benefits impacting everyone from the individual living in Norwich, to the corporations who operate out of London, is still beyond comprehension to me. I won't give up my UK citizenship, as some have suggested; I will ensure my family and I have a right to stay in our adopted country through applying for permanent residency. I will ensure that my young son will have the option of living in Austria for as long as he wants to while the dust settles in his home country and educate him to understand that his vote is important in all matters of politics and that he can be the change the UK needs.

Antony Martin, Austria

★★★

Life in Europe for a 12-year-old boy

My name is Oakley Martin and I am 12 years old. I happened to be living in Europe when Brexit began. At first I didn't seem to be bothered about it because I kind of knew that the votes wouldn't be high enough for Britain to exit the European Union. However, when the votes were in I was flabbergasted to see on the news that the people of Britain really wanted to leave the EU. One of my friends in school called Oscar Hetzinger produced a 6 week inquiry on Brexit and only then did I notice how much of a big deal Brexit was to not just the EU but the world too.

My opinion on Brexit was all nationalities could be together; in the end we are all one huge family stuck together on one surface, arguing and fighting for practically nothing. The people in control of voting and electing really need to sort out their priorities. In my point of view, Brexit is becoming more and more stressful and digging a hole that Britain can't climb out of.

Oakley Martin, Austria

★★★

As a British/Romanian family there is no certainty wherever we go. My husband and baby daughter are Romanian, my son has a birth certificate in both countries and myself and my eldest daughter are British. They aren't welcome in England and we have an uncertain outlook anywhere in Europe.

The racism following the vote became too much for my husband to bear. One week he was laughing with his work colleagues and the day the vote was announced, they were telling him to go home. Having a Romanian surname through marriage meant I suffered the same treatment.

My husband speaks fluent English, better than some Brits to be fair! We were stood in the aisle of a popular supermarket and he was talking to me and our children. A couple were stood behind us, heard his accent and tapped my husband on the shoulder. They asked him where he was from and he said Romania. "F★★k off back where you came from you dirty thieving b★★★★★d. We don't want your sort in our country. We voted to get all you foreign f★★★ers out. Why are you still here?" was the response he received. The woman turned to me. "You had children with this man? People like you need putting down. You're a dirty f★★★ing wh★re."

I wish I could say that this was an isolated incident but it wasn't. They became daily occurrences. Our once tolerant country had turned into a racist hell, literally overnight.

My husband never claimed a penny from the UK. He always worked and paid his contributions as did I. We paid into our pensions. What will happen to those after Brexit?

We and our children deserved more than the toxic environment our world had become. We took a gamble and left the UK for Romania in April 2017. I had spent 26 years in the UK and my husband 10. We sold up our entire lives and left with a trailer of possessions.

We are now totally dependent upon my husband to support us whereas in the UK I could find employment at the drop of a hat. I worked in the legal field – UK Law which is no use to me in another country.

I will have to study the language and then return to college and study for a new profession. That takes a lot of time and money to achieve. We don't know what will happen after Brexit. Is it worth studying at all?

Our daily lives are uncertain. We will never return to the UK. I'm ashamed to say that I'm British. Britain today is nothing like the Britain I grew up in and thought I'd raise a family in. What will happen to my family if myself and my daughter are shut out of Europe? Where will we go? Where can we be together as a family? Why should we have to worry all the time about what will happen to us? I know there are many more people and families like us, in the UK and across Europe. We are the ones the Government doesn't care about. A gambling chip as it were and the ones that will pay the highest price if it all goes wrong.

Hannah Vişan, Romania

★★★

I am a 59 year old ex NHS nurse living in France with my wife and 4-year-old daughter.

I bought our house in France in 2006, initially as a project and holiday home. In 2013, I decided to take early retirement from the NHS, after working 22 years as a Registered Nurse for Learning Disabilities, and move lock, stock and barrel with my wife and then 3-month-old daughter.

We did this because we could exercise our right of free movement and felt that we could provide a better life for our daughter, while enjoying the benefits ourselves.

Since being here I have seen how much the EU invests in our area of France, from restoration of our local 13th century church, building new roads and building a new swimming pool in our local town. The investments from the EU are proudly displayed – this never happened in the UK, it was if any grant from the EU had to be secret because the Government wanted to look good!

Since the referendum in 2016 our lives have changed immeasurably. I have written to MPs, Lords, MEPs, European Commissioners, Heads of States and negotiators in our quest to be heard.

My retirement has been put on hold to fight this ridiculous situation that we are in. Not for my sake, but my daughter's, and her generation, who will not have the same opportunities that we had, and had absolutely no chance of a say in the direction of their future.

I have learned that most of our elected representatives, at the moment, don't care about the plight of their constituents. When writing to them about the Human Cost of Brexit, we had very few personal responses. Some were misinformed about our situation, most had not even considered how much we were affected, and by 'we' I mean EU citizens in the UK as well as UK citizens in the EU, and just spouted the party line.

What has affected me most though is how a referendum designed to heal the rift in a UK political party has managed to completely split the country. No matter what happens from now on around 50% of the population will be angry. It has caused my fellow citizens to become insular and unaccepting of others.

I am proud to be British, but I am ashamed of the road my country has taken, and the casualties caused along that road by ignorance and prejudice. My father served in the army for 22 years and his father fought in the 1st World War, being decorated at the Somme and spending a great deal of his later life in an asylum because of it. This was not what they served for, they served for a more tolerant, inclusive society.

I am lucky enough to live in an accepting and inclusive country such as France and will jump through every hoop put in my way in order to stay here, but feel very bitter towards the politicians that have put me, and millions of others, in this position when it would have been oh so easy for them to say to the 3 million people who have made the UK their home: 'We will guarantee your present rights, thank you for what you have contributed to our society, we are proud to call you citizens of the UK.'

I can only apologise to all those affected, and say to them all – the UK Government does not speak for me, neither does the so-called popular press who demonise honest, hard-working people, nor the racist, ignorant bigots who target innocent children.

I only hope that my voice, and that of like-minded people, can be loud enough and heard by enough people to stop this madness.

Michael Harlow, France

★★★

I am Scottish, British and European. Being born in 1975, I was raised on metric measurements, red passports and Erasmus exchanges. The Treaty of Maastricht was coming into force as I came of age, so my parents and school teachers encouraged me to study French and German. Europe was the future.

Just after the Ukrainian Orange Revolution, when Europe was still opening up, I met my husband (a Dutchman) on a train from Kyiv to Bucharest. By 2014 we were starting a family, so I agreed to move from Oxford to the Netherlands. We were blasé about the decision, assuming we could move to the UK at a later date. That was our plan when Brexit struck.

Brexit went against everything I was raised to be. The practical effects are unpleasant: civic status thrown into doubt, future plans cancelled or put on hold, any British savings losing fifteen percent of their value overnight. However, the emotional toll has been worse. Uncertainty is the new normal, and for the first time, I feel a conflict between Scottishness and Britishness. I am not a nationalist by nature, and the upsurge in 'British' nationalism worries me. Scotland did not vote for any of this.

To their credit, the Dutch government has never made Brits in the Netherlands feel uncomfortable, despite the rights of three million EU citizens living in the UK being used as bargaining chips. However, returning to the UK with my Dutch family was out of the question in the aftermath of Brexit, so I redoubled my efforts to integrate into Dutch life. Dreading Geert Wilders, I joined a Dutch political party and knocked on doors in our village. My family bought a home with a garden and I tried to put down roots. However, for all the positives of Dutch life, I remained homesick. My husband agreed to move to the UK, but only once the status of EU citizens, both current and future, was resolved.

Like most of the five million whose lives have been turned upside-down, I scoured the British media for signs that a pragmatic solution was being found. Towards the end of 2017, progress seemed to have been made with (apparent) agreement on Phase One of the negotiations. Sadly, that consensus has already unravelled. The shambles that has accompanied that unravelling makes me ashamed to be British. Our Government does not give a stuff about all the lives thrown into turmoil. They don't even seem to value the Good Friday Agreement.

In February, I attended a wedding in Western Australia. I have spent wonderful times there in the past, and, on hearing of my Brexit troubles, my Aussie friends suggested that my family move Down Under for a while. The bureaucracy involved in moving to Australia is no small matter, but at least the rules are clear. It could be years before there are clear rules for EU citizens moving to the UK. We are no longer willing to live with the uncertainty.

I never intended to leave the UK permanently, but now have no idea when I will return. I am a citizen of nowhere.

Alison Smith, the Netherlands

★★★

In January 1999, Monique, whom I had met 5 years earlier, came over from France to live with me in London. Although she had stayed in England when young, had liked the way of life there, and was fluent in English with no accent, she was unable to find a job, despite her impressive qualifications and references. It seemed to her that she was being rejected as a foreigner.

This was made even clearer when somebody kicked her car because it was French, and another driver swore at her. This demonstrates that xenophobia in relation to EU citizens was already there long before Brexit.

Monique moved back to France in 2002 having found a good job there. I waited until March 2008 before joining her, when I had reached 65 and was in receipt of my state and private pensions. France has been an attractive place to retire to, and I hope it continues that way. Although assurances from the UK Government suggest that it will, there's a great uncertainty hanging over everything, which is most unsettling. The important aspects for me are to continue receiving my UK pensions every month, and to continue having S1 healthcare cover.

For me, obtaining French citizenship is not a realistic option: my language skill is rudimentary, my involvement with French society is minimal, my knowledge of French history and culture is sketchy. Following the advice of Christopher Chantrey in a Lords' committee hearing, I went through the process of applying for a Carte de Séjour UE/EEE/Suisse Permanent, valid for 10 years, and was relieved to receive it after 8 weeks: this should simplify obtaining whatever is required post-Brexit to remain in France.

That testimonies in the book "In Limbo" make for disturbing and distressing reading is a gross understatement. That EU27 citizens already settled in the UK, especially those with families, have not yet been given unqualified and unconditional rights to stay and work in the UK permanently makes me ashamed of my homeland.

Membership of the EU allowed me to move to France, where I feel freer than I ever did in the UK. It's looking like I should be able to stay in France, but this is by no means certain. What's certain is that I'm in no hurry to return to Britain, and Monique is, of course, against it.

George, France

★★★

I still remember being woken up early on the morning of 24th June 2016. I felt as if I had been punched hard in the stomach. I don´t remember such a strong combination of anger, shock and disbelief ever before in my life.

I grew up as an expat kid, born in Sudan, my father was a vet in the Colonial Service and we lived in about 4 places over the 6 years he was there. After independence we moved back to Ireland for a while before going back to Africa again.

Across the EU I have lived in Ireland, UK, France, Netherlands, Spain and Portugal and worked in many other EU and EEA countries.

My freelance career has been built around the support of cooperative relationships, largely in business, but also in other fields. It is much easier to destroy cooperation than to build it. As an inspirational colleague once said: "Cooperation works, but it takes hard work" and is very easy to destroy when people no longer see the big picture, focus on self-interest and become fearful of trusting others.

I feel ashamed of the UK government and the small island mentality that is producing Brexit. I am appalled at the open xenophobia that is increasingly visible and I am saddened by how easily the hard-won benefits of international cooperation have been damaged by the whole Brexit process.

The impact of Brexit on me has already been considerable and will get worse. It has made me much more politically aware and more progressive in my thinking and actions.

Our apartment rental business will almost certainly lose a large proportion of UK clients and I have already lost 20% of my UK State Pension value. I will find it increasingly difficult to get work across Europe. I am seriously worried about the climate that my grandchildren in UK will grow up in and their likely loss of e.g. Erasmus opportunities.

Rory, Portugal

★★★

I am British by birth and by lineage, I can't say that I have ever been particularly patriotic – it has always seemed nonsensical to me to feel proud of a country, town or district just because of an accident of birth. I loved the wild scenery in West Yorkshire, where I spent the first few years of my life, and I loved the excitement and cosmopolitan feel of London, where I spent most of my adulthood. I can love living somewhere, sure. But to feel proud of it, proud to be a Yorkshire woman, an adopted North Londoner, an Englishwoman, a Brit? That concept is alien to me, and as far as I can remember, always has been. However, until 2016, I never felt ashamed of my country of origin.

Something else in my past which I believe is relevant to my current mindset: immigration. Between my somewhat exclusive (and, of course, all white) school and the local town was, at the time, an area "notorious" for being the home of Commonwealth immigrants from Pakistan, people who had been invited to the UK to fill unskilled jobs, but who were, nevertheless, despised and feared in their host country. We girls were repeatedly told never to walk through this area.

When I moved to London, I lived in an area which was very culturally diverse. My next door neighbours were Turkish origin on one side and Italian on the other. Other ethnic minorities in the area included Somalis, Ethiopians, Greeks, Jamaicans, Barbadians and South Africans. We all seemed to get along fine.

Until I was in my mid-forties I never gave much thought to being European. I had never been talented at languages so my holiday journeys to mainland Europe included little contact with the "locals". However, living in London as a single parent with a young child was becoming increasingly problematic, not to mention expensive, so in 1995 I applied successfully for a job with an agency supporting the British army in North Germany. Suddenly, there we were – living in Europe! It soon became apparent to me how insular we Brits are, huddled together on our little island, thinking the world revolves around us. My son and I quickly adapted to being British-Europeans, accepting that "home" was wherever we were living at the time.

Twenty one years passed... my son grew up and moved away – not back to the UK; he was always clear he would never make his home there again. I wasn't sure. I had married and bought a house in Bavaria, had semi-retired but continued to teach English as a second language. I saw the UK as a place I might live should I ever be left alone. I would affectionately describe quirky little "Britishisms" to my English conversation classes, give them recipes for Yorkshire pudding and shepherd's pie, bring in British food for them to taste (they were always very polite!). I would use the Union flag to signify that in our classroom we should only be speaking English... and yes, in a sort of distant way, I suppose I felt positive about being British-European.

But then that fateful morning came. I must have felt more British than I had thought, because I was shattered when I heard about the Brexit vote. We met a group of German friends that day and I could hardly meet their eyes, I felt so ashamed. They couldn't believe the result and couldn't understand why I had no vote in my "own" country. They asked questions I couldn't answer – why had the UK decided to leave a successful trading partnership where even countries that had had problems were now stabilising? Why weren't the Brits working together with other Europeans to strengthen and change the EU rather than leaving for uncertainty? Couldn't they see that peace had been achieved in Europe through the union? And more personally, would I be able to stay in Germany? If I couldn't, would my husband be able to live in the UK? I was worried – and still am – about my eligibility for health care in Germany. Although I have lived here for 22 years, when I worked with the British army I wasn't registered in Germany. I have only officially lived here since 2012 so may be ineligible for citizenship until 2020. I haven't paid into their health system and am now nearly

70. Will the Germans want to take responsibility for an ageing immigrant? Because of my history, I have friends all over Europe. Would I still be able to visit them freely, without applying for visas every time? I was suddenly clear that I never wanted to live in Britain again. I was ashamed to be British. Ashamed that British people had fallen for hate propaganda about immigration and for obviously false promises from far-right politicians. How could this have happened?

I've heard rumours of Europeans in the UK being badly treated. Then I went to London to visit my sister-in-law. We were speaking to each other in German on the street and a passer-by swore at us and told us to "go home". I gladly did. But for my sister-in-law, London is home. And I'm afraid I want nothing more to do with it.

My husband and I recently attended a British training course. There was a frightening amount of anti-European sentiment. Also, there was a lot of talk about "immigrants" in Britain and the need to have tight borders – how women can no longer walk the street for fear of being murdered, raped….sounds familiar? Being from a criminology background, I checked, I really did, on crimes perpetrated by immigrants. No higher than the indigenous community, all sources seemed to agree, other than for crimes that were immigration related. But the confusing thing was, the "immigrants" being castigated were Somalis… the last time I looked, Somalia isn't a part of the EU, or even of Europe. Or have I missed something? Oh, I was told, but Mrs Merkel let all those asylum seekers in (good for Mrs Merkel, I privately thought, but kept that gem to myself). But hang on, she let them into Germany, not the UK. The UK can and always has been able to decide on how it deals with non-EU arrivals. But this stuff was beyond all logic. The only sympathetic ear we had was from an Irish couple understandably unconvinced about how the border with the north could remain open after Brexit – and very worried about the implications of this.

I've now applied for German nationality. I have a statement from my previous employers stating that even if not registered, I have indeed been living in Germany since 1996. We are now only waiting for a statement of income from our tax advisor. I am hoping against hope that soon I will be able to travel as a German – I won't any longer have to be identified at borders as British. I'm still not sure what will happen about my health care, but when asked where I come from at least I will be able to say Germany rather than Britain. I expect that many Brits will see me as unpatriotic (yes!) and traitorous. But that doesn't worry me. I won't feel "proud" of being German any more than I felt "proud" of being British. But at least I won't any longer have to feel ashamed of my nationality.

Chris Atkinson-Price, Germany

★★★

My father was an economic immigrant. In 1969 he accepted a job in Zambia because his work prospects in our home town of Grimsby were so poor. Our whole family joined him there in 1970. I returned to UK to live with my grandparents and attend school just over one year later. I well remember, a year or so after that, sitting with my Nana and Grandad in their candlelit kitchen in front of a gas oven with its door open to provide heat, listening to the battery-powered wireless as the electricity was turned off for the night. This didn't last long but it was a clear sign that the UK was a basket case and the experience made a deep impression on me.

During the time that I lived with them, my Grandad lost his long-term job at a paper mill and all he could find to replace it was work as a labourer on Grimsby docks. My Nana continued to work as a school cleaner, employed by the Council. Neither of them had rights to anything beyond their (joint) State pension.

To my conscious knowledge, the three most significant things that have happened in the UK since my secondary school years have been: UK joining the 'European project', in its early form as the EC; development of the North Sea oil & gas industry and deregulation of UK finance services (the 'Big Bang'). All of them have, to varying degrees improved the lives of UK citizens. We haven't always got what we wanted from any of the three but, in my experience, we've always been a net beneficiary. I know that my grandparents would have benefited from Workers' Rights.

It's ironic that the third thing, the Big Bang, is probably the one that has created greatest wealth for the UK. Oil & gas certainly helped to keep the lights on but didn't bring the wealth promised and is a transient thing as we know. At the same time, these changes in banking and financial services probably also created the greatest divisions; between North and South and between 'haves' and 'have nots', specifically in England. I have reflected on this a great deal since the EU referendum campaign started and those divisions began to be exploited by some of the people who have benefited most from the thing that caused them. There were very good reasons for the Leave vote on 23 June 2016, but most of them had little to do with the UK's membership of the EU.

In the months after 24 June 2016, I was convinced that the UK Government would say to 'the people': "We recognise and understand your pain. We have let you down and need to put much right. But, if we actually go ahead and leave the EU we will not have acted in the best interest of the UK or its people." This didn't happen and I still really don't understand why. There is little point theorising as to the reasons in this testimony.

Last year, having never been actively involved in politics before in my 57 years, I was moved to raise a petition calling for MPs to be allowed to vote freely upon whether Brexit should be cancelled. I felt so strongly about the subject that I cycled over 700 km from my current home in France to deliver that petition to 10 Downing Street. So far, it has not been successful but I am still hopeful. I really did this for my first grandchild, (Maeve), who was born in October 2016, because if she is ever sat in front of a fire with her Grandad in future, he wants to be able to tell her that he did everything he could to stop the UK leaving the EU and denying her the benefits that he and her father had enjoyed. He will also be able to tell Maeve that her Great Grandad, (who is now back living in Grimsby), was ashamed that many of his fellow UK citizens seem to have voted Leave because they didn't want people to benefit from being economic migrants as he was.

Paul Hearn, France

★★★

I have had a lucky life. I was brought up in London in a stable and loving family, and educated in good state schools, giving me the foundation and support to get to university. After graduating and spending a couple of years travelling, I returned home to look for work in the late 80s. The job market in the UK at that time was not good. The incumbent Tory government's infamous advice to the jobless was to get on your bike. So I did.

My bike took me to Aberdeen, Scotland to work offshore in the oil industry. My career progressed quickly and took me to the Middle East, many parts of Africa, Norway and, most recently, back to mainland Europe. Again, I have been fortunate that the industry I chose (fell into) pays well, and for the majority of my working life I have been a higher rate tax payer. Despite working abroad for large periods of time I have never avoided paying tax because I passionately believe that a fair taxation system is the foundation of a fair society.

I don't know what will happen for me personally (I have just moved to Bucharest with work after 5 years in Vienna). I know that non-EU citizens in my company have huge obstacles getting work permits and many will not be able to extend their current contracts. So I guess the worst that can happen is I lose my job and have to return to the UK. Certainly my situation is nothing compared to others, and some of the stories I have read of non-British EU citizens living in the UK.

I voted Remain, therefore, because I wanted my country to be part of the future, to be part of the bigger ideals of the EU, but also because I firmly believe being a member benefits us all.

In return for my position I have been labelled a snowflake, a Remoaner, and a traitor. I have been told that living where I do is a lifestyle choice and if I don't believe in Britain I should leave and live in Europe (which, ironically, is what I want to be able to continue to do!).

So what are my feelings now? I have to confess, I have an overwhelming urge to say "fuck it". To fully immerse myself in the "me, me, me" society, I'm OK, Jack. And then watch the people who voted Leave "to get their country back" lose their jobs as the few remaining factories we have move to the EU, leaving them with zero-hour fruit picking jobs.

But I refuse to give in to this negative feeling. I want my country to be one I can be proud of. I want to be able to say I'm British, holding my head up and not apologising. I want us to return to the welcoming society so evident just a few short years ago during the London Olympics. I want people of all other nations, EU and beyond, to want to come to my country because they know British values mean they will find a fair and inclusive place to live.

At the moment, I can feel none of this. I no longer recognise the UK. It is very hard being ashamed of your own country. The UK will be worse off in many ways after Brexit, but for me, whatever happens, the lasting damage will be from the unleashing of a grubby nationalist underbelly, and how we have treated the EU citizens who have made their homes and built their lives in the UK. Someone asked me recently if I would retire to the UK? For the first time I hesitated. I don't know if I want to any more. But when that time comes, after the UK has so disastrously turned its back on the international community, I'm not sure who else would want an immigrant Brit.

Neal Whatson, Romania

HOPE

I never thought of myself as a particularly emotional or angry person before the referendum on 23rd June 2016. To say that the result was a shock to me would be a massive understatement. Not only was I stunned by the vote, but by the reactions of those on both sides of the argument. How I reacted personally was also something I was totally unprepared for. The feelings of anger, sadness, depression and disbelief swept over me in waves, and I found myself bursting into tears at random moments, and doing a lot of shouting & swearing. Those feelings lasted a full 3 weeks, and it really was like a grieving process, but without the acceptance phase. 20 months on, I still don't accept the result, and I never will.

The only thing that preserved my sanity during those first weeks was finding fellow sufferers amongst my friends, both real & virtual. I don't think any of us truly appreciated what we stood to lose until the prospect of it being snatched away was right under our noses. I can assure you we appreciate it now!

Something snapped after 3 weeks, & I determined to get myself out of my funk and to take some action. At first that was getting to grips with what was happening, avidly reading the newspapers (not something I was in the habit of doing), and sharing information on social media. Having never had any interest in politics previously, I soon became an addict, devouring everything I could that was Brexit-related. That addiction now equates to 70 hours a week, 7 days a week, and I'm an active campaigner. I do not intend to stop campaigning until Brexit is cancelled.

Living in Spain for the last 10 years has inevitably changed my relationship with the UK to some degree. Brexit, though, has changed my feelings towards my home country and my fellow Brits quite significantly, perhaps irrevocably. I was always proud of the British qualities of tolerance, openness, and common sense, but now I just feel shame. I would like to feel pride in Britain again, as I take pride in being European, but I'm not sure if that wound will ever heal. The way that European citizens have been treated in the UK is absolutely shameful – I don't know if they will ever be able to forgive us or trust us again. I feel I want to apologise personally to every single one of them. If Brits in Europe were treated half as badly, there would be an uproar.

I have to pinch myself some days when I realise just how much I have learned, the new skills I now possess, even including public speaking. Those new abilities, along with the wonderful new lifelong friendships I have made are the only positives of this whole sorry mess. I have surprised myself that at the age of 64, I am working harder than I have in my entire life and that I have a passion and drive for this cause that I didn't know I possessed. That passion, along with a real sense of hope and optimism, have seen me through some very dark days. I have to believe that the UK will come to its senses before it's too late. The alternative doesn't bear thinking about.

Sue Wilson, Spain

★★★

Before that bravado referendum, something niggled me. Why weren't we being told what would happen to us, and the non-British EU citizens in the UK, in the event that Leave 'won'? The vote mysteriously went from being advisory to binding. Apparently, the government leaflet delivered to all households said so. (I didn't get one. I live in Italy.). There was still no mention about the fate of several million 'displaced' citizens. Thus, those permitted to vote, unwittingly or otherwise, were made party to the government's failure to protect all of us. That somehow made it very personal. I felt like I'm being punished, written off even...

A book I was reading in the run-up to June 2016 has made a lasting impression on me: "This Boy", Alan Johnson's memoirs about his tough childhood in London's North Kensington. Despite the squalor, it talks of great fortitude. But it was also the setting of the Notting Hills Riots in 1958; gangs turned on West Indians who'd arrived under an immigration policy. "Into our decaying streets they came, scapegoats for overcrowding...", said Johnson. Sound familiar? What erupted was some of the worst racial violence ever in Great Britain. Judge Salmon, when sentencing, proclaimed: "Everyone, irrespective of the colour of their skin, is entitled to walk through our streets in peace, with their heads erect and free from fear. As far as the law is concerned, you are entitled to think what you like, however foul your thoughts; to feel what you like, however brutal and debased your emotions, to say what you like, providing that you do not infringe the rights of others."

Those last words helped me understand why I felt so affronted by the referendum. But worse than that, I sensed a dark chasm opening up... All the progress made fighting discrimination, since those pivotal events of 60 years ago, seemed to have disappeared into the ether. 4.5m people are being treated like some form of underclass, most of all, by the lawmakers of the land who are supposed to protect us! Those pillars that underpin democracy have buckled. Imperfect as it is, I realise now why democracy is so important. To hold fair elections (and referendums), to treat all citizens equally and protect their rights... these are the fundamentals that make people feel included in society, and safe, not only in a physical sense. Even those being British elsewhere need to know, come what may, their basic rights are secure.

I hate to see what is going on in the UK now, and shudder with shame every day. An uncaring *let's pretend* government continues to neglect crises such as housing, the NHS, emergency services... Ever larger sections of the media, increasingly pernicious and unfettered, are scapegoating people and inciting hatred...

But the well-thumbed pages of my book also tell uplifting stories of resilience, determination, compassion for others, and triumphs against all the odds. I'm optimistic. When the UK disconnected me, I became connected with others, who were adrift in a scary wilderness like me. We're not united by any particular political persuasions, but a common belief that everyone has a right to live free from fear, included and respected. We need to knit those lost 60 years back together again.

Clarissa, Italy

★★★

Some of my earliest, and fondest, childhood memories are of southern France. It was here, at the age of two, that I spoke my first words of French, to the elderly lady who owned the local bar *tabac*. For this effort, I was rewarded with ice cream, and from then on I made an effort to speak French whenever the opportunity presented itself! It was also at this point that I fell in love, not just with France, but with travelling. I love interacting with people from different places, finding out about different conversations, and the EU has made this so much easier than it was before. So, that explains the root of my emotional attachment to Europe, and to the EU.

But freedom of movement is so valuable! Freedom to live, work, study and travel to 27 countries, with a whole multitude of different cultures and peoples. It is a freedom that we value, a freedom that we have grown up with, and a freedom that many of us will be sad to lose.

When tuition fees were tripled to £9,000 per year in 2010, I was furious. Unfortunately, as a ten-year old, I did not know any words strong enough to describe the anger and hatred I felt towards the government responsible. It's alright, I told myself. You'll have Europe. So

I started some research into tuition fees. £9,250 per year in Britain, £1,700 in the Netherlands! Europe seemed to be the perfect option: adventurous, away from home, a chance to fulfil my dream of living abroad, and a total saving of around £21,000. That dream is still, just about alive for me, but what about next year? What about my sister, who is in the first year of her GCSEs, or my twelve-year-old cousin? What an opportunity they will miss out on because they were born too late! There is also talk that school exchange programmes might disappear. Aged fourteen, I spent ten days in Göttingen, Niedersachsen with a German family, and had a brilliant time. It boils my blood to think that the short-sightedness, idiocy and racism of, let's face it, the older generation may deny those opportunities to whole generations of young people!

And the most galling part of this? We didn't get a say. We didn't get a vote on our own future.

To the oldest generation I say thank you. They fought and defeated fascism, winning peace for the whole of Europe, and then founded the EU to cement that reality! My own great-grandfather would turn in his grave if he could see what was happening now. Unfortunately, I was only eleven when he died. A veteran of El Alamein, a liberator of concentration camps, and a lifelong Conservative, he was also a committed Europhile. His core argument was that, despite its faults, the EU kept peace in Europe for fifty years.

I feel ashamed of my country. Growing up, I was taught tolerance and open-mindedness. Coming from such a wonderful, diverse, multicultural country has always been a point of pride for me, but I sat up and watched that die overnight. I woke up in a country I took great pride in, and went to bed in a country I wanted nothing more to do with. And so, so many of my friends felt the same. I remember on the Tuesday talking to a friend who had stayed up most of the night, and neither of us could say anything. We were both so crushed by the result, so shaken that a campaign based on racism and xenophobia had won over the British people.

However, I got a rather pleasant surprise earlier. A lot of the people I regularly talk politics with are very right-wing and quite socially conservative, and I was beginning to worry that support for the EU among young people had been overestimated. A few conversations later, and I was much happier with the picture. Everyone I had asked, all of them seventeen or eighteen years old like me, had expressed positive views of freedom of movement, and many seemed to think it was a stupid question. "Of course I like freedom of movement! Who wouldn't like the ability to freely explore an entire continent?" The pro-EU sentiment has not gone away; in fact, I believe it is getting stronger. If we are dragged out of the EU against our will, mark my words, our mission will be Bre-entry. If young people harness the opportunity to dictate British politics for the next ten years, it is the Europhiles who will win. As Alex Salmond said after the Scottish independence referendum: "For us, the dream will never die." For the young, it is a dream of re-joining an open, social Europe. I firmly believe that enough young people are ready to take these attitudes and these words into round two for us to defeat Brexit. I just hope it happens soon.

Thomas Haynes, United Kingdom

★★★

As a child, I experienced a degree of suffering and so I decided that my mission in life was to fight the suffering of others. I studied Law with French because I thought being a lawyer would be a way to help people. But that wasn't enough, and so, given that I was good at French, I decided that a career in international human rights would be the way to go. So I started doing internships in Brussels working in EU affairs

266

establishing myself in the human rights sector. I got accepted for a traineeship at one of the official agencies of the EU and was the social media advocacy trainee for the EU Agency for Fundamental Rights.

Someone with my skill set should be fighting to promote British values abroad, making sure we do have a say in the world, but because of the inequalities in my own back yard, I have to fight to fix those problems instead. The failure of British governments to work in the interest of all Brits pushed people to vote for change. For me, it's not about my loss of opportunity. It's that I'm not being used properly. I should be defending human rights both in the UK and across the world. Instead I'm stuck making economic arguments so my country, the country that birthed me, raised me and taught me all I know doesn't permanently wound itself.

When the vote happened I felt a sense of failure. That we'd failed as a country. Like when an empire falls, which is ironic, as many Brexiters saw it as a way to rebuild the empire. But now I feel driven and determined because I can see how all the arguments against Brexit can win, and I know I have the skills and soon the platform to deliver them.

Femi, 28, UK

★★★

In many ways I'd rather paint than write – words can be manipulated and twisted, sentences cut to invert their intended meaning. I'd use black and charcoal grey, a big gruesome smudge, and maybe some red – nothing like the green meadows and bountiful seas we've been told to believe in.

Looking back to 23 June 2016, it seems like my last day of innocence. My last day of believing that Britain was respectable. I was here, on a nearby island. In the morning, I went to the post office to buy a stamp for a postcard to my parents. "Za Veliku Britaniju", (To Great Britain), I said to the elderly lady behind the counter. "Je li to u Europskoj uniji?" (Is that European Union?), she asked. "Today yes, tomorrow I'm not sure", I replied. It must have sounded flippant, making light of fate.

Later, back on the mainland, I sat up all night, watching the results arrive in real-time, constituency by constituency… astonished… because I'd followed the Scottish independence referendum in a similar way, but that came out all right. It was dawn when I went to bed. I awoke around noon with a horrible feeling of loss, as if someone had died. Then I remembered – I was an "orphan" now. It all seemed so impossible and unreal and hopelessly absurd and unnecessary.

Friends here were kind and understanding, though some people looked at me slightly askance, as if suspecting maybe I'd gone mad too, like the rest of Britain. I hadn't, but I was stuck in a vacuum of disbelief and disappointment. After three days, one side of my chin swelled up. The dentist said it was an infection, gave me antibiotics, and warned an extraction could be imminent. One week later, the swelling was gone and an x-ray showed nothing untoward. "Strange" said the dentist. But I knew what had caused it.

Oddly, Croatia has prepared me well for this mess. The break-up of Yugoslavia saw the end of Tito's "Brotherhood & Unity" project. What ensued was disgusting and in reality nobody won – each former republic has lost more than it gained through independence. Criminals profited, politicians lied, the media stoked fear.

Nationalism is a vile illness, the domain of the petty-minded and resentful. But unscrupulous politicians use it to fill the void, the emptiness that people feel when they no longer believe in themselves, nor the state, nor God.

Immediately after the referendum result, I blamed the outcome on "lack of education" (not to be confused with lack of intelligence). The British have always had a peculiar anti-intellectual streak and it has proved to be their undoing. As far as I'm concerned, the EU was founded on peace and cultural understanding, and Britain should be proud to be part of it.

This morning I started my painting. Besides the black, grey and red, it will have sprouts of green – because I still believe we might remain.

A., Croatia

★★★

My husband and I, who are both British citizens, live in a small village in France. Our children were both born in France but are, currently, also British passport holders.

Kemplich is situated near the borders with Germany, Luxembourg and Belgium. Between 1871 and 1918 our village was in the area annexed by Germany. In 1939 the inhabitants, who spoke the local Germanic dialect were evacuated to the West of France, where they were not able to communicate with the families which were ordered, at short notice, to house the refugees.

On Saturday morning last summer, we celebrated my eldest son's 11th birthday with his friends from the local French school. He chose a trip to our nearest swimming pool, in Merzig, Germany. This was followed by pizzas and cake at our house. The children, aged 7-11 spontaneously sang 'Joyeux Anniversaire'; 'Happy Birthday' and 'Guten Geburtstag'. German is compulsory from the age of 6 and next year they will start English, although several of them already attend private lessons organised by myself.

In the afternoon, our family participated in a ceremony at the Hackenberg Fort, built as part of the Maginot Line to defend France from invasion by the Nazis. The event marked the inauguration of a guided path explaining the history of the fort to ensure that the events of over 70 years ago are not forgotten. Along with volunteers from the Amifort Association which runs visits to the fort, in English, French and German; the event was also attended by representatives of our local, departmental and regional government.

My husband is part of the team of guides at the fort and all four members of our family played music as part of the ceremony. My seven-year-old son was chosen to hold the ribbon for the official opening. Along with my husband and some of our French friends, he was also very proud to play his trumpet for the European Anthem, Ode to Joy.

It was a lovely weekend, with lots of quality family time and happy memories. But this is not why it was important.

It was important because it emphasised the true meaning of the European Union.

The EU is not about quotas and subsidies and regulations. The EU is about friendship and cooperation; understanding; building bridges; cultural awareness. And most importantly, it is about working together to make sure that our children, throughout the continent of Europe, grow up in peace.

Helen Hodgson, France

IN LIMBO PROJECT – BLOG

Please keep on reading, on our blog, **https://inlimboproject.org**, more of our compelling testimonies. We were so inundated with wonderful testimonies for this book that unfortunately there wasn't space for those listed below. A VERY SPECIAL THANK YOU to them. For those who gave consent, you will find their testimonies on our blog:

A.L.M., Spain
Anna, France
Anna, Ireland
Anna Gruffydd, Italy
Anonymous, Europe
Anonymous, Italy
Anonymous, Portugal
Anonymous, Portugal/Switzerland
Anonymous, Spain
B., France
Ben, Germany
Bill Bamber, Finland
Brenda Henderson, France
Brian M., France
Carol Fraser, France
David Reiling, Peyia, Cyprus
Elspeth, France
George Holmer, Belgium
Grazia, France
H., Germany
Helen Moore, France
J., UK
Jackie Hale, The Netherlands
Jacqui Charles (née Shaw), France
James Barisic, France

Jay, United Kingdom (aspiring to move to Sweden)
Jayne Hamilton, UK
J.B. Rowbottom, Italy
Jim Byrne, France
John, Belgium
K., France
Karen, France
Kate, France
K.G., Spain
Kristina Howells, France
Lawrence Renaudon Smith, Spain
L.P.S., Barcelona, Spain
Mary Guttel, Hungary
M.C., The Netherlands
M.D., France
M.J.G., The Netherlands
Nick O'Brien, Germany
N.L., France
Oliver Rowland, France
Pam, Spain
Paul Blackburn, UK
Polly Ernest, Hereford, UK
R., Germany
Ray G., France
Rebecca, UK
Samantha, The Netherlands
Sian Shaw, Spain
Sue Maddox, France
Tom Cassidy, Spain
Tracey Runciman, Germany
Yvonne, France

THANK YOU

This book would not have been possible without the help and support of some very special people.

Our most sincere gratitude goes to:

Professor A.C. Grayling for his moving foreword;
Alice Harrey for the book cover that expresses so well what our book is about and for the book design;

To the *In Limbo Too* core team, and in particular:

Jan Glover and Carole Convers who have worked tirelessly behind the scenes and without whom the production of this book would have been a lot less smooth;

To Stephen Corsham for helping with the proofreading;
To Véronique Martin for suggesting the word "too" to the title;
To the administrators of In Limbo - Our Brexit Testimonies and Brexpats - Hear our Voice for their wonderful support.

Thanks also to the other groups who contributed to this book with their testimonies and in particular to:

Jane Golding, Chair of British in Europe and the whole steering team and core member groups; Kalba Meadows representing RIFT (Remain in France Together) and group members; Sue Wilson, Chair of Bremain in Spain and the group members; Molly Williams from Young European Voices; Roger Boaden and ECREU; Sarah Parkes and the team from British in the Netherlands; Sarah Pybus and Neal Whatson representing British in Romania; Rory Stewart and British in Portugal.

Our friends
the 3million, Scientists for EU, The 48% and many other groups;
Jean Lambert MEP, Molly Scott Cato MEP, Seb Dance MEP, Julie Ward MEP, Catherine Bearder MEP;
Lisa O'Carroll *The Guardian;*
Oliver Rowland *The Connexion;*
Rebecca Morris-Buck *Conversations with Europe;*
Claudia Delpero *Europe Street News.*

Thanks to those that have helped us by sharing and donating to the crowd-funding page.

Finally, a special thank you to all the wonderful people that trusted us with their testimonies. You speak for all of us and we hope that this book will touch hearts and open minds. The "In Limbo Project", of which the book *In Limbo Too* is part of, is an example of pan-European cooperation at its best, showcasing what people can achieve when working together across borders, to achieve a common goal and a unified voice.

Elena Remigi (In Limbo Project) and *Debbie Williams* (Brexpats – Hear our Voice)

Printed in Great Britain
by Amazon